£10-

D1144855

LL SAINTS PARK

NORTHERN ACCENT

*The Life Story of
the Northern School of Music*

Hilda Collens
by Ray Howorth

Northern Accent

The Life Story of
the Northern School
of Music

JOHN ROBERT-BLUNN

ALTRINCHAM
JOHN SHERRATT AND SON LTD

First published 1972 by
John Sherratt and Son Ltd
Altrincham

© *1972 John Robert-Blunn*

ISBN 0 85427 029 9

Made and printed in Great Britain
at the St Ann's Press, Park Road, Altrincham
Cheshire, WA14 5QQ

Preface

In the beginning, one of the nine students was Doris Euerby and for fifty-two years she has worked with loyalty and devotion for the Northern School of Music. What is now the end is the beginning of the Northern College of Music and we look back with pleasure, and forward with joy, to a united ensemble in which the Friends of the past, present, and future will maintain and strengthen the traditions of good work and goodwill. In writing this book John Robert-Blunn has paid tribute to many of these Friends and in our turn we place on record our appreciation of his work in writing the Life Story of the Northern School of Music.

IDA G. CARROLL

Prelude

All music colleges resemble one another, but each is unique in its own way. This short book, which is more of an extended essay than an attempt at comprehensive compilation, sets out to record the main events in the life of the Northern School of Music and to indicate why it is unique. To what degree it is unique the reader must judge, but there can be few other colleges which have been founded (unwittingly) by a woman, which have had only two principals (both of them women), and which have preserved so successfully an atmosphere of warmth and friendship.

The Principal, Miss Ida Carroll, asked me to write this story and it could not have been done without her untiring help in pursuing facts, documents, school records, and letters, and in answering my barrage of questions. Miss Carroll also gave me encouragement and much hospitality whenever needed, and was ready with advice on the many occasions I asked for it. That kindness, which I acknowledge gratefully, will show the extent to which this book may claim to be "official". Miss Carroll suggested many improvements and I accepted some of her suggestions, but the responsibility for the facts, stated or omitted, and for the views expressed is mine.

To Miss Doris Euerby I am greatly indebted for lending me irreplaceable material and for her reminiscences of Miss Collens and the early days of the school. I have also received much help from Miss Irene Wilde, Miss Eileen Chadwick, and Mr Geoffrey Griffiths. The school magazine, published annually since 1937, has been of invaluable assistance and I have made much use of material written by the editors Mary Dunkerley and Dorothy Pilling, and by various other contributors. I also wish to thank Mr Michael Sherratt, of John Sherratt and Son Limited, for his guidance and forbearance; Mr Harold Riley, for his readiness to help; Mr Michael Kennedy, for permission to reprint extracts from his admirable and authoritative study "The History of the Royal Manchester College of Music, 1893–1972", published by Manchester University Press; Mr Thomas Pitfield, for permission to print the verse he composed on the occasion of the stone-laying of the Northern College of Music, Manchester.

Acknowledgement is also made to the Editor of *The Guardian* for permission to reprint extracts from the *Manchester Guardian;* to Lancashire and Cheshire County Newspapers Ltd for permission to quote from the *Manchester City News*; and for permission to quote from *The Music Teacher.*

I have also drawn briefly from other published sources, including *The Pianoforte,* by William Leslie Sumner (Macdonald, revised edition, 1971); *Keyboard Musicians of the World,* by Percy M. Young (Abelard-Schuman, 1967); *The Great Pianists,* by Harold C. Schonberg (Victor Gollancz, 1965). I thank their authors and publishers.

It is only when one comes to make a list that one realises just how many people have helped in the preparation of a brief chronicle. Many more could and should be named. An all-embracing expression of gratitude is simply not good enough, but it will have to serve. I have been lucky in having the counsel of friends, colleagues, and acquaintances who played their parts anonymously. That, alas, is true of the book itself. Many names are omitted because the temptation to catalogue them has been resisted wherever possible. Teamwork has always been the essence of the Northern's life story. In telling it the aim is to be neither exhaustive nor exhausting, but to be concise.

JR-B

Manchester, 1972

Contents

Illustrations

CHAPTER ONE

Hetty

Behind many acts that are thought ridiculous there lie wise and weighty motives.—La Rochefoucauld

Hilda Hester Collens was a lively and intelligent child. At boarding school near Wrexham in North Wales she applied herself enthusiastically to her studies and to many school activities. With the zeal and dedication which were to mark everything she did until the end of her life, she would often get up at six o'clock in the morning so that she could have extra time in which to practise the piano.

Her first love was music. Or was it? Certainly, from a very early age she had an ardent desire to teach, and it was an ambition she worked towards with determination through her youth and she succeeded despite parental opposition—perhaps even because of it.

Hilda, born on September 24, 1883, was the fifth and youngest child of Arthur Collens, a banker, and his wife. Hetty, as Hilda was known to her family and close friends, was particularly close to her twin brothers, Frederick and Arthur. While Hetty was still very young the death of Frederick came as a great shock. The boys had gone skating on Rostherne Mere in Cheshire and Frederick was drowned. Arthur was rescued.

The tragedy was held to be responsible for a nervous "tic" and a slight hesitation in speech which Hetty had ever after. Mr Collens, a practical businessman, saw these as impediments to a teaching career, and he urged his daughter to give up the idea. She, however, was determined and she had her way. There was a compromise: Hetty began her teaching career at Hazelwood, the family's home in Broad Road, Sale. At first there were a few pupils who came for piano lessons.

Often they would return to Hazelwood to join Hetty and Mrs Collens in happy musical evenings. Soon after, Hilda Collens began teaching at Sale High School for Girls. Her piano lessons there were so successful that the headmistress, in mock despair and real tribute, said that all the senior girls wanted to take up a musical career!

Hilda Collens joined the Manchester Association of Teachers which was headed by Dr Walter Carroll. The decision to join the association was significant because it brought her into contact with kindred spirits anxious to improve teaching methods. During the association's 1909–10 season Miss Collens heard a lecture by Tobias Matthay on musical appreciation. Matthay, born in London on February 19, 1858, was a fine pianist who had studied at the Royal Academy of Music, where he became professor of the piano. Matthay had decided views on piano-teaching methods and these he expounded in several books, including *The Visible and Invisible in Pianoforte Technique* and *The Act of Touch*.

True to the German blood in his veins, Matthay did a thorough job. Harold C. Schonberg[1] says that Matthay "broke down the elements of piano playing into a fearful system. We learn that there are six ways of arm functioning : poised-arm element, the forearm-rotation element, forearm weight, whole-arm weight, forearm down-exertion, upper-arm forward-drive. We learn about touch-forms, weight-touch, touch-construction, weight-transfer, rotary relaxation, rotation stresses, duration-inflections." Indeed, the Matthay System was not without its jargon; nor was it without its successes. Among many leading pianists who were pupils of Matthay were Harriet Cohen, York Bowen, and Irene Scharrer, whose cousin Myra Hess was to become the most famous of Matthay's students. Myra Hess, still in her teens, had made her concert debut only two years before Hilda Collens heard Matthay lecture in Manchester. Like so many other musicians and teachers, Hilda Collens was greatly impressed by Matthay

[1] *The Great Pianists* (Gollancz).

who, according to Percy M. Young,[2] "performed a very great service in demonstrating that a more reasoned approach to the mechanics of playing would make for better, and more musical, playing." The foundation of the Matthay System was, says Young, "the necessity to use physical energy in the most economic manner. The secret was relaxation." This, too, was the main theme behind the teaching of Matthay's German contemporaries, Rudolf M. Breithaupt and Dr Steinhausen, an army surgeon who studied the muscular movements involved in playing various musical instruments.

Matthay's theories came at the end of the nineteenth century, a time when music teaching was moving out of the doldrums, and when piano technique was beginning to receive the attention it deserved. Whatever criticisms are now levelled at the Matthay System, there can be no doubt that it provoked thought, encouraged changes for the better, and produced many fine pianists. A concise account of Matthay's main theories has been given by William Leslie Sumner[3] :

> Relaxation was sometimes misunderstood. Briefly, it meant the use of intelligent economy in the effort of sound production: it told of the evils of "key-bedding", for when the hammer has left the mechanism, no further pressure on the key can affect the tone; and if the note is to be held down it should be done with the minimum of effort to keep it down. Matthay insisted that his pupils should "play upon the strings" and "think through" to the actual source of the sound. . . . Matthay preferred hard hammers in his pianos, for these would encourage the touch to become more sensitive. He would never allow his pupils to hit down a key or to attack the keyboard from a height. He realised that fortes are not absolute, but only relative to the accepted level in the particular circumstances of quiet playing. The decibel gain, from soft to loud, is that which is accepted by

[2] *Keyboard Musicians of the World* (Abelard-Schuman, 1967).
[3] *The Pianoforte* (Macdonald, revised edition, 1971).

the ear, not the energy output of the fortissimo. Matthay realised that piano tone tends to lose its beauty if its dynamic level is too high.

Matthay, says Sumner, "always made technique subservient to musicianship. His method was an obvious reaction against the German muscular and heavyweight techniques." And so, inspired by Matthay's lecture in Manchester, Hilda Collens approached the great man and asked if he would take her as a pupil. He agreed and, while continuing her own teaching, Hilda Collens was soon travelling regularly to London for lessons.

Matthay was the catalyst in her career, but it was another pioneer, Walter Carroll, who was to play a more sustained part in her development as a teacher, and who was to give practical help and friendly advice.

He was born at 156 Ducie Place, Strangeways, Manchester, on July 4, 1869, the youngest of five children and the only son. He was mildly interested in music, but when he left Longsight High School at the age of fourteen he became an office boy. At the age of seventeen he had to give up work because of a serious illness. A visit to a church on Easter Day, 1886, during his convalescence, proved to be a turning point, for there was a fine organist and a good choir: Carroll wanted to learn music. As his health improved, he began to attend evening classes in harmony and composition given by Dr Henry Hiles and in 1888 won a Hargreaves Music Exhibition at Owens College, Manchester.[4] The following year he began to study piano and composition privately with Hiles and in 1891, at the age of twenty-two, became one of the first Mus.B.s of Durham University.

The year 1892 was eventful. He became organist and choirmaster at St Clement's Church, Longsight, he was appointed music master of the Training College, and two of his piano sonatinas were published. Among those impressed

[4] He gained a second award of the Hargreaves Exhibition in 1891.

by the sonatinas was Sir Charles Hallé, who was then in the process of founding the Royal Manchester College of Music. Hallé sent for him and offered him a place on the staff as lecturer in harmony and counterpoint, of which the professor was Hiles. At 10 a.m. on Tuesday, October 3, 1893, Carroll, who was then only twenty-four, gave the very first lecture at the new R.M.C.M.

In 1896, the year he married Gertrude Southam, he took a second Mus.B. degree, this time at the Victoria University of Manchester (of which Owens was now part), and four years later he became the first graduate to gain by examination the degree of Doctor of Music at Manchester.

Hiles retired from the college in 1904 and Carroll was appointed his successor as principal professor of harmony and composition. He was also appointed lecturer in music and examiner for degrees at Manchester University, a post also vacated by Hiles that year.

Carroll was particularly interested in the training of teachers. In 1907 he had founded the first Manchester training course for music teachers, a course which continued until 1918, and in 1909 he became the R.M.C.M.'s first professor of the art and practice of teaching. His salary was £120 a year.

A former student, Dr Charles T. Lofthouse, was to recall[5] Carroll's work at the college. He said: "His classes were memorable experiences. . . . We were called to give demonstration lessons in front of the class. I remember we had to make a list of good points shown by the teacher, as well as the less good ones. I recall the kindly criticism he gave of a lesson. It was: 'He tried to tackle too many points in the time. Better to attempt to do one thing well.' How true this is!"

Carroll had always been interested in Church music and frequently deputised for the organist at St James's Church,

[5] Address given at the Carroll centenary service held at the Musicians' Chapel of the Church of the Holy Sepulchre, Without Newgate, London, on July 6, 1969, where the east window depicting the Magnificat had been dedicated to Carroll's memory in 1957. The window was presented by his daughters.

Birch-in-Rusholme (Birch Church). When in 1916 the choir-master of Birch was killed on active war service Carroll became honorary choirmaster and director of music there. He continued at Birch for twenty-two years, during which time he championed the right of women choristers to wear cassocks and surplices on terms of equality with the choir men. It was a cause quickly taken up at St Ann's, Manchester, and at many other churches. It should be noted that he was not advocating women's voices for the melody, or soprano, part, for which he considered boys' treble voices more suitable in providing a lead for the congregation. He regarded women's voices as excellent for the alto part.

He was good at training choirs. One chorister during Carroll's time at Birch said: "He made the practice sessions so interesting that one had to be ill before one ever thought of staying away." In that event a note to Carroll was necessary, or he would be round at the chorister's house to find out the reason for absence. "Words of censure and words of criticism were delivered in a very dignified way." Meticulous attention to detail was one of his characteristics, whether in training the Birch choir, in his handwriting, or in keeping scrapbooks of cuttings on musical subjects. He dressed neatly and soberly in starched shirt, dark jacket, waistcoat, and "elegant striped trousers". His work at Birch, however, belongs to the future, as does his great work as music adviser to Manchester education committee; but when Hilda Collens first met him in the early years of the century he had already made his mark on Manchester's musical life and was particularly active at the Royal Manchester College of Music and the Victoria University.

By joining the Manchester Association of Teachers, Hilda Collens had been introduced to the vigorous, adventurous world of Tobias Matthay and Walter Carroll and many other distinguished musicians, including Stewart Macpherson, who was also destined to have a profound influence on her career. Like Carroll, Macpherson was a pioneer. Like Carroll, he was a Lancastrian, born in the rival city of Liverpool in 1865.

Unlike Carroll, he seems to have decided on a career in music at an early age, and with this in mind, went to the Royal Academy of Music, where he was a brilliant pupil and afterwards a respected professor.

Macpherson was a sound conductor and composer, but he put all his energies into widening music appreciation. He held that "the true appreciation of music by the community at large can only come about by means of some systematic endeavour, on the part of musicians, to present the best examples of their art in such a way as to make clear to all and sundry that in such things there is really some element of greatness and truth which it is *worth while troubling about*" [his italics].

He maintained[6] that "besides more obvious qualifications, the true musician, executant or teacher must

(a) possess a good first-hand knowledge of musical works— a knowledge not confined to those for his own special instrument or voice;

(b) know something of the growth and development of the musical art and of the chief characteristics of the best composers, through close contact with their music."

"The musicianly musician," he added, "must be both craftsman and artist." And although a musician's craftsmanship might be beyond reproach, he might never have "blossomed into the *artist*, in the deeper meaning the word".

Macpherson urged students to remember that

. . . all our technical acquirements—even the Practical Musicianship which rightly claims much attention today— are no more than varied aspects of craftsmanship. Such craftsmanship, vital as it is, however, must not be the end of our efforts, but a means to a greater end—music itself. Whether we are playing or singing, or whether we are giving our attention to the playing and singing of others, or perchance are trying to make acquaintance with some fine

[6] Magazine of the Matthay School, Manchester, No. 4, July 1940.

work by a silent perusal of its pages, the approach is the same; it is the "hearing ear" alone—the ear that really *preceives*—by which (to use the words of a quaint but far-seeing old teacher) we ultimately get to "the music of it."

Although Macpherson was "a musician with a capital M" he "knew as much about art as he knew about music." He believed that musical training should be on a much wider basis than was usual at the beginning of the century. Part of his campaign for musical appreciation was the advocacy of "aural culture", which now has long been an accepted element of serious music training. Frederick Shinn's ideas on "ear training" had been gaining acceptance since 1899 when the first volume of *Elementary Ear Training* was published. Shinn's second volume appeared in 1910. In collaboration with Ernest Read (born 1879), another Matthay disciple, Macpherson worked on the three volumes of *Aural Culture Based on Musical Appreciation,* of which the first was published in 1912.

Macpherson was a born campaigner who understood the close relationship of the various art forms, including painting, sculpture, poetry, prose, architecture, and music. He was a gifted pianist with huge but sensitive hands and he had a prodigious memory. He was also a brilliant lecturer who "talked very learnedly but made it very interesting". He would usually illustrate his lectures by playing from miniature scores, although how much he owed to his prodigious memory and how much to his prodigious sight-reading skill is now anyone's guess.

Hilda Collens was attracted by Macpherson's ideas and she began to take lessons in harmony and musical appreciation from him. The inspiration she found from this teaching, and the friendship they established, lasted until the end of Macpherson's life. Miss Collens was fortunate to have found such friends right at the start of her career. They reinforced her will to succeed.

CHAPTER TWO

Teachers All

The gift of teaching is a peculiar talent, and implies a
need and a craving in the teacher himself.

—John Jay Chapman

When war broke out in 1914 Percy Waller, Matthay's representative in Manchester, responded to the call of patriotism
and enlisted. Matthay asked Miss Collens to take over the
tuition of the students and, again despite opposition from her
father, she did so, giving up her pupils at Sale High School
for Girls and at home. She had the counsel not only of
Matthay but also of such friends as Carroll, Read, and
Macpherson.

Carroll's own crowded career was at a crucial stage of
development. The training courses for music teachers, which
he began in 1907 at the Onward Hall, were continuing with
teaching demonstrations and lectures by experts. The courses
were very popular: the *Manchester Guardian* recorded that
"during the first session 127 teachers of various ages and
experiences joined the class, the average attendances at the
20 lectures being 95. In the second session the membership
rose to 157 . . .".

At the Royal Manchester College of Music, Carroll, with
other professors including Egon Petri, Rawdon Briggs, and
Carl Fuchs, had been active. The board of professors had
urged the appointment of external examiners. Michael
Kennedy, in his history of the college,[1] says that the board
"also passed a resolution preventing any teacher from being
an examiner of his own students in the diploma (teachers)
examination". The college council refused to accept this

[1] *The History of the Royal Manchester College of Music 1893–1972*
(Manchester University Press, 1971).

resolution. It did, however, agree to several suggestions made by Carroll and his colleagues for placing greater importance on the teaching diploma, and on March 31, 1909, under the chairmanship of E. J. Broadfield, the council decided to set up a new department for the special training of music teachers. Reporting the scheme, the *Manchester Guardian* said:

> The Manchester College [R.M.C.M.] will offer a complete course of instruction extending over two years, and comprising lectures, discusson, and actual practice in teaching. The scheme is largely the result of the efforts of Dr Walter Carroll. . . .
>
> Discussing the methods of teachers in the past and at present, Dr Carroll expressed his strong opinion that they have to a very large extent been misdirected. Instead of doing his utmost to develop the talents and sympathies of the pupil the average teacher—and often the parent of the pupil, he adds—thinks mainly of preparing for an examination. "My own opinion", he proceeded, "is shared by perhaps all the eminent musicians in Manchester—namely, that there is too much examining in music especially of young children.
>
> As a whole, genuine local examinations in music have spread a wide knowledge of sound classical music, but they have been carried to excess, and in a vast number of cases the teaching and the learning have followed lines which, apart from the examination, were not best calculated to develop a real love of music in the pupil. With a better training of music teachers, bringing their methods more into line with those of the best teachers in other branches of education, I see no reason myself why "local examinations" should continue to exist. . . .

Carroll declared that it was impossible "in a solitary interview lasting some fifteen minutes to judge of the real capacity of either teacher or pupil".

He continued:

The higher examinations held in London, such as for the diplomas of A.R.C.M. and L.R.A.M., come, of course, under another heading. They are not a hindrance to the musical development of the young, but more in the nature of a hall-mark for those whose studies are nearing completion, and who are of an age when preparation for one examination will not have the same cramping effect as the constant struggle for certificates, which too often occupies most of that period of childhood which should be regarded as a glorious opportunity for building up a love of music for itself, and the development of the natural musical instincts and tendencies which every child possesses in a greater or lesser degree.

The new department opened on October 7, 1909, and in March of the following year the *Manchester City News* said:

A new era in music teaching is in progress, the result of a movement which, if it had not its inception in Manchester, this city has been the first to put into practical shape, namely, the teaching of music teachers as distinguished from students.

The importance which the newspaper attached to this movement can be seen from this further extract:

Some time ago a Bill was unsuccessfully promoted in Parliament for the registration of music teachers. On going into this matter it was demonstrated that even those holding the foremost positions as performers, or the highest musical degrees and diplomas, had little real title to the designation of teacher, in that they had not received any definite training in the art of teaching music. Clearly Parliament could not grant facilities for the protection of a class which had no prima facie evidence of possessing the knowledge it wished to have protected. The leading musical institutions at once introduced into their professional examination schemes questions on the art of teaching, and at one, at least, of the London institutions systematic lessons, with practical demonstrations on a class of children provided by arrangement with the London County Council, were given.

On this occasion it was a case of Manchester's doing today what London did little more than think about yesterday, for the *Manchester City News* went on:

The honour of providing existing teachers of music with opportunities for bringing themselves into line with this new movement belongs to Manchester.

The newspaper then pointed out the success of Carroll's training courses, noting that in the 1909–10 session just ended the lecturers had included Carroll himself; Matthay; Mrs Annie Jessy Curwen, daughter-in-law of John Curwen, founder of the Tonic Sol-fa method of teaching sight-singing; Robert Jaffrey Forbes, a fine pianist and organist, and a member of the R.M.C.M. staff; and John Acton, who was one of the first members of the college staff.

The courses were receiving influential support and, although "conceived as an experiment, proved feasible and instructive". The *Manchester City News* concluded: "The movement has commended itself to teachers in other parts of the kingdom, and already classes on similar lines are being formed in London and elsewhere."

On this occasion the *City News* did not mention the new department of the R.M.C.M. Carroll did so the following week (April 2, 1910) in a letter pointing out, first, that another course had been arranged at the Onward Hall for the following autumn and, second, referring to "the public-spirited step which the Royal Manchester College of Music has taken in establishing a department for the training of music teachers". It differed, Carroll wrote, in three important aspects "from any attempt yet made elsewhere to meet this pressing need". The points of difference were that it was a regular course of seventy-two weekly lectures and demonstrations covering two years, that the teacher's diploma could be gained only by those who had, during three years' studentship, completed this two-year course, and that the course was not optional "as in other institutions which give some few lectures on teaching".

Carroll moved to his peroration : "Gradually to substitute the trained teacher for the untrained is a work full of glorious possibilities for the art of music. That the Royal Manchester College of Music is the first institution to make this training a compulsory part of its curriculum is a fact deserving of the widest recognition."

Among Carroll's first students in the new department was John Wills, aged sixteen, one of Petri's piano pupils. Carroll was perceptive ; he described Wills as "most promising in every way, especially as regards thoroughness". Wills gained his performer's diploma with distinction and in July 1911 took his teacher's diploma. Later, he was to win the college's Hallé Scholarship and, in 1915, the Dayas gold medal. Wills's subsequent career, both as a pianist and a member of the R.M.C.M. staff, confirmed the soundness of Carroll's judgment. Another Petri pupil was Dora C. Gilson, whom Carroll described as "a fine musician" with "a good temperament for teaching". She went on to do important work at the college, teaching singing and piano, later becoming a member of the college council.

There were many others who came under Carroll's influence at the college, not only when he was professing harmony and composition, but from 1909 onwards in the new department. Kennedy writes[2] :

The new department—"somewhat of an innovation in the equipment of a college of music"—was a success. In those days, teaching of music was regarded as a respectable profession but performing it in public as a professional was still "not quite the thing" as far as most middle-class families

[2] ibid., p. 34.

were concerned, so it is not surprising to read that "the great majority of students" became teachers after leaving College and that many teachers unconnected with the College applied for admission to the new classes.

Carroll joined the college council in 1915 (the year after Hilda Collens—whom we have purposely neglected for the moment—had taken over Matthay's students in Manchester). Manchester Corporation's representative on the council at that time was Councillor Will Melland, a member of the city's education committee. Melland was another who was impressed by Carroll and his ideas, and in 1918 was instrumental in securing his appointment as part-time music adviser to the committee. Melland sponsored the appointment, personally guaranteeing the salary for two years.

That year Carroll began more pioneering work, this time by organising music appreciation classes in Manchester primary and secondary schools. The classes came four years before Britain's first broadcasting service, nine years before the British Broadcasting Corporation was established by royal charter, and long before radio could play an effective part in the development of musical taste.

Life at the R.M.C.M. seems to have become increasingly irksome for Carroll, whose powerful personality inevitably brought him into conflict with some members of the staff, including Dr Thomas Keighley and R. J. Forbes. Keighley, a former student, became a staff member in 1898 and a member of the council in 1917. A difference of opinion between Carroll and Keighley developed in 1913 over the appointment of a junior teacher in harmony. Carroll's nominee for the post was the twenty-three-year-old Henry Baynton-Power, a talented pupil first of Petri and then of Frank Merrick. While attending the two courses in the department of teaching he had made a good impression. Carroll noted that teaching was Baynton-Power's first interest, remarking: "Exceptionally gifted in Music and Personality. Also, a rare addition, fine reliable Character, including a perfect sense of honour. Has every qualification for a fine Teacher." On Carroll's recommendation Baynton-Power got the job.

Carroll does not appear to have been able to get on with either Keighley or with Forbes, of whom Kennedy has written[3] : "Loveableness was not his most apparent characteristic, for he was a man who successfully concealed his feelings and his enemies regarded him as a past master of intrigue. He was highly principled, a shrewd administrator, wise investor and a first-class musician." Carroll, too, was highly principled, shrewd, and a first-class musician. He seems to have been more dynamic than either Keighley or Forbes, or even Stanley Withers, the college registrar, whose relations with Carroll were cool.

The clash of personalities and Carroll's dissatisfaction with the way the college was being run at that time led to a serious quarrel. Carroll and another council member, Mrs Norman Melland, objected to the proposed reinstatement of a foreign professor, who had been absent from Britain during the war years, over the man who had remained and done good work. Carroll and Mrs Melland felt it was unfair to the present teacher and, on this matter of principle, they resigned from the council in 1919. In 1920 Carroll resigned his college posts (professorships of harmony and composition, and of the art of teaching) and those at Manchester University.

Even after all these years there are those still under the impression that Carroll quarrelled with the college and, failing to get his own way, went off to found a rival or "breakaway" music school of his own. It may, indeed, be true that he failed to get his own way (it is fascinating to contemplate what might have transpired had he stayed on at the R.M.C.M!), but the rest of the argument does a disservice to the facts, sadly underestimates Hilda Collens, and grossly overestimates the importance, in its early years, of the small academy which she founded.

[3] ibid., p. 79.

Walter Carroll had been on the R.M.C.M. staff since it began work in 1893, a total of twenty-seven years. He had not been a ship that had passed in the night and when in 1920 his appointment as Manchester's (and England's) first full-time music adviser was confirmed, his influence on the city's educational and musical life became even greater.

According to Percy A. Scholes,[4] Carroll had "deliberately sacrificed a university career for a school career, left to others the care of the talented few and turned his thoughts and energies to the needs of the many". He was now able to concentrate on teaching children, the "establishment of the teaching of Music in the Elementary Schools of Manchester as a fundamental subject of the curriculum", and the composition of music for children.[5]

While Carroll was campaigning and pioneering, Hilda Collens was continuing her work with Matthay's students. As we have seen, she had a passionate interest in teaching and she was sympathetic to the aims of Matthay, Macpherson, Carroll, and the enlightened movement which was then gathering momentum. She shared the beliefs of Macpherson, her friend now and still her mentor in musical appreciation and harmony, and wished to put them into practice. Individual piano lessons according to the celebrated Matthay System were not enough for Miss Collens, who was also a regular attender at Carroll's Onward Hall classes and very much in touch with the new ideas and theories. She discussed with Macpherson the idea of broadening the scope of the training offered to the Matthay pupils. Such a step would involve starting her own school and coping with all the extra problems this would bring. Macpherson, always a staunch friend, assured her of his support. Carroll also promised to help.

Hilda Collens next approached the parents of potential music students. Only a few were interested, but enough to encourage Miss Collens in her foolishness.

[4] *The Music Teacher*, June 1934.
[5] Yet another aspect of his career. Nearly five million copies of his music for children have been sold so far.

CHAPTER THREE

The Nine

It is the mark of a good action that it appears inevitable in retrospect.—Robert Louis Stevenson

Nine girls from the Manchester area turned up at the small studio over Hime and Addison's music shop in Deansgate on Wednesday, September 22, 1920, and were greeted by Miss Collens. The students present at that very first weekly assembly were

> Kathleen R. Bostock
> Doris M. Euerby
> Doris K. Fox
> Audrey Gomersall
> Audrey Ifor-Davies
> Margery Pilkington
> Beatrice M. Rollins
> Alice Thompson
> Sylvia Vallance

The school week was then, curiously enough, from Wednesday to Tuesday but terms were to end on Fridays, so giving the students an extra half-week's tuition. The weekly assemblies of the full school, addressed by the Principal, developed into a tradition which—despite vast growth in the number of students—has never been broken. Another tradition, which also began on that very first morning and has never been broken, was that the Principal takes all full-time students at least once a week for aural training. At first, with only nine students, neither the assembly nor the aural classes put very much of a burden on the enthusiastic Hilda Collens but— apart from absences because of illness—she continued them as the school grew and until the day she died. Her successor kept up these traditions.

27

The atmosphere was friendly. Miss Collens knew all the girls and used their first names. When Doris Euerby had played for Miss Collens at a preliminary audition that summer "she immediately called me Doris, although if I had been going to any other place I would have been 'Miss Euerby' from the word 'go'. Well, this suited me down to the ground, because I didn't feel like 'Miss Euerby' at all at that stage."

Miss Collens was reserved almost to the point of shyness. She may have been self-conscious about the hesitation in speech which became manifest when she was nervous or under stress or on the rare occasions when she revealed annoyance. Her father had been right in thinking that she would find the business of public speaking something of a trial, but she was determined to overcome this handicap. After such occasions as the annual distribution of awards, when she was obliged to make public speeches, she was happier when she was out of the limelight. On more than one occasion she was overheard to comment: "Thank goodness that's over." The slight nervous twitch of the head was another handicap with which she came to terms.

How could such a person found a school of music? One can imagine Mr Collens putting the question. And to her other apparent handicaps may be added her femininity and the primness which went with it. Ladylike in all things, she must have seemed, to the conventional male world of 1920, an unlikely candidate for any serious artistic or commercial success. That such a frail bundle of fastidious zeal should attempt such things! At best she was likely to achieve only a very limited success. There was, perhaps, a touch of the Jane Austens about her little school—cosy, harmless, and always well-mannered.

But Hilda Collens, though she would never do anything so outrageous as cut a bread-roll with a knife or scoop up her peas, and though she would diligently observe the conventional manners of the time, was not to be influenced by what outsiders thought of her ideas about music-teaching. "Once she had made up her mind to do something she would have done it if the world had fallen about her", said Irene Wilde, a former student who later became one of Miss Collens's staff. Doris Euerby said: "Miss Collens didn't seek the limelight: she rather did the very reverse. What she wanted to do was to improve the standard of training teachers so that the teaching of music would be ever more efficiently taught. All her time and attention, all her thought, was focused on this."

It was this dedication which led her to start her own academy and try out in practice the theories to which she had been attracted. The emphasis was still on the piano, but the scope of the school was widened. Miss Collens, too, ardently wished to extend the range of musical appreciation, to improve teaching standards, and to do something more than produce proficient keyboard technicians. Technique, of course, is important, but there is much more to musicianship than that, as Hilda Collens realised. Starting with the first nine students she was able to concentrate on her life's work.

It is unlikely that she realised that she was founding an important school of music that September day in 1920. Whereas other schools may have armed themselves with a rich array of well-known patrons and taken unto themselves a constitution before opening their doors, Hilda Collens had just nine students without benefit of the laying of a foundation stone or the ceremonial of an official opening ceremony. The only help she had in teaching the nine was given by Mildred Esplin, who had studied at the Royal Manchester College of Music. The two young women had met in the lift of the Onward Hall when they were leaving one of Dr Carroll's classes for music teachers, and later they had become firm friends. They worked together in the Manchester branch of the Music Teachers' Association and in 1919 they had founded a holiday course on music which became an annual event. Now, in 1920, the two friends were again working together in the new venture.

The next problem was finding a name. Characteristically,

Hilda Collens modestly discounted using her own name. She could have used it without affecting the chances of success, for her small group of students had been attracted by Miss Collens alone. She, however, preferred instead to ask Matthay for permission to use his name. He agreed readily and the assortment of musical young ladies in the small studio over Hime and Addison's became the Manchester branch of the Matthay School of Music.

The little school prospered. Without any visible means of financial support, with only one room, a settee and a piano, the little group of young women set about their studies. It was a small, close-knit community in which friendships grew, a family presided over with maternal kindliness and generosity by a warm-hearted spinster. Hilda Collens's personality served as an inspiration to them all. Her generosity became evident in many ways, most of them untold, including (in at least one early case) free tuition in return for token secretarial help— which may or may not have been needed—and which was additionally rewarded by the gift of a fountain pen.

Hilda Collens was a dedicated teacher and a dedicated musician. She was also a dedicated Christian. While living and working at Sale she was an active church member and on Sundays her teaching talents were applied to propagating the Gospel. Throughout the week she practised what she taught at Sunday school. She had faith, and it was this which sustained her throughout her life. So strong were her religious convictions that, had she been forced to choose between teaching at Sunday school and teaching music, Sunday school would probably have come first. Fortunately, no such choice was necessary and the influence of her Christian beliefs was felt in the everyday life of the Manchester branch of the Matthay School in an atmosphere of good fellowship and goodwill. With Hilda Collens religion went deep.

It was not long before Hilda Collens realised that the small studio she had rented was inadequate if the school was to develop. After only a year it was clear that her foolishness might not have been so foolish, that her idealism was matched by pragmatism, and that faith is a formidable ally. She had other allies. Macpherson, who held similar strong religious convictions, continued to be a source of inspiration and a wise counsel. Ernest Read, a fine musician who was professor at the Royal Academy of Music and who had studied with Matthay, was another important ally. Walter Carroll was another.

The first year, then, passed off smoothly, but Hilda Collens was not complacent. She began looking for larger premises. She found them quite near, in the Tudor Galleries at 79 Deansgate. Three rooms were available. They were rather dark—electric lights were on most of the time—but there was space to expand. Miss Collens and her students moved there in 1923. The move inspired confidence in the Manchester branch of the Matthay School: there was no depression in that house and, as for the possibility of defeat, it did not exist. There was an increase in the number of students. A secretary was needed and Jessie Coombs was appointed and so helped to ease Miss Collens's burden of administration. The wider interests of the school were reflected by the appointment of Gertrude Riall to teach singing and Kathleen Forster to teach the violin.

The school atmosphere grew in friendship and intimacy despite the modest increase in numbers (augmented by a few part-time juniors), and when Hilda Collens needed recruits to the staff she had only to look to her own students. Former students appointed during the five years at the Tudor Galleries included Kathleen Bostock, Doris Euerby, Beatrice Rollins, and Annie Warburton. There was also the first resignation, when Mildred Esplin left on her marriage to Arthur R. Moon. A training course for teachers was started and Frank Roscoe, secretary of the Royal Society of Teachers, inspected the work and as a result "the course was recognised as efficient and accepted for the purpose of registration".

While the Matthay were finding their feet, Walter Carroll was settling in as Manchester's music adviser. Very soon after-

wards Manchester education committee created a music
scholarship and in 1924, on Carroll's advice, it was awarded
to a young pianist, Irene Wilde, who was enabled to begin
studies at the Matthay School. It was a controversial decision,
for it seemed that ratepayers' money—£60 a year for three
years—was being used to swell the (non-existent) profits of the
commercially minded Matthay. As Irene Wilde's grant was
intended to cover the cost of books and music as well as
tuition, her arrival would not have increased the school's
profits by any significant amount, but there were some who
felt that Irene Wilde and her grant should have gone to
the Royal Manchester College. Carroll, who would not be
deflected by controversy, laid himself open to allegations of
favouritism and even of spite. There is, however, no sensible
reason for supposing that such a man would have risked his
reputation merely out of spite: it would have been completely
out of character.

He had been impressed by Miss Collens and her work and
he recognised the distinctive warmth and friendliness of the
small Matthay community in Manchester. It is likely that
he considered Irene Wilde would be happy there. He was
right.

The Christmas of 1926 found Miss Collens and her staff
busier than ever. Once again the school was on the move and,
once again, the move was just along Deansgate, this time to
premises at No. 260, next door to the Milton Hall. It was
completed on January 5, 1927. The school now had a concert
room, so that it was possible to extend the choir, start orchestral
and ensemble classes, and hold more frequent practice-recitals
and lectures—in fact, to do many more of the things expected
of a school of music! Because there was more space it was
even possible to found a school library, tended first by Mary
Dunkerley and Marjorie Jones, and later by Molly Hibbert.
It was good to have five rooms, an office, and the concert
room, but there was one additional luxury. This was a small
electric cooker which gave heat for small meals and hot water

for making tea. A feminine touch. Miss Collens might work her staff and pupils as hard as she worked herself, but she knew the value of a timely cup of tea.

The practical problems of space had been solved, at least for the time being. There remained the problems of the school's educational and artistic development. The bias, of course, was towards music in general—it was first and foremost a school of music—and towards the piano in particular, but the range of subjects was wide enough to ensure that students received a good general education.

English and elocution classes had already become an established part of the curriculum. Students were expected to be as articulate in speech as in music. Hilda Collens, who never completely vanquished that slight nervous hesitation in speech, would have been keenly aware of the benefits of the elocution classes for her students.

Now that there was room for ensemble classes, Harold Warburton, professor of the 'cello, was anxious to start an orchestra, but the difficulty lay in finding enough instrumentalists. Like the rest of his colleagues, Warburton was a pioneer whose enthusiasm was not to be damped down by such trifling considerations. Two or three violinists, one viola player, and one 'cellist were found and practices began. There was no-one to play the double-bass and, indeed, the school did not possess such an instrument. One was needed before the school could think seriously of an orchestra, so a bass was purchased. Ida Carroll, daughter of Dr Carroll, had enrolled at the school in 1922 at the age of sixteen and had become a fine pianist. She now tackled the double-bass.

Warburton's zeal soon infected this small band and the first results were encouraging. Membership grew and the original quintet became an orchestra. Warburton continued for three years, creating and maintaining an *esprit de corps* so typical of the school then and now. Growing professional commitments caused Warburton to give up these orchestral classes and his place was taken by Archie Camden, the

C

bassoonist. It was not long, however, before the B.B.C. claimed Camden's services and the Matthay School had to find another conductor.

They did not have to look far. William Rees was in Manchester and he agreed to take the orchestral classes, consolidating the work already begun by Warburton and Camden. The orchestra, giving regular concerts, had become part of the Matthay establishment. Orchestral "teas", provided by a different player each Tuesday, also became a school tradition. To record the development of the orchestra and the fact that it was not very long before the school had no fewer than five competent orchestras is to anticipate events, but it is evidence of the continued expansion of the school's activities. Under the inspired direction of Gertrude Riall the school choir was doing well with the foundation work which was to make it pre-eminent among choirs in the Manchester region.

Just before the move to 260 Deansgate, Jessie Coombs, the school's first secretary, retired because of ill health. Hilda Collens, busy as a hard-working principal, needed a secretary who would also be her lieutenant. It was an important post requiring, among other things, tremendous drive, imagination, an infinite capacity for hard work, and ability to cope with the relentless routine of administration, as well as the usual secretarial qualities of tact, discretion, efficiency, and a readiness to work with and for the boss. The secretary was also required to dust the pianos.

Miss Collens decided to offer the job to a girl she had auditioned four years earlier (playing the Schubert A flat impromptu, Opus 90, No. 4) and whose promise as a pianist had been fulfilled. Ida Carroll received the letter on the day she heard she had passed her final examinations. She was then twenty and had misgivings about dusting the pianos, but she wanted the job and she accepted.

(Carroll's other daughter, Elsa, also took piano lessons from their father, but her career took a different course. For forty-five years she was chief clerk to the Joint Matriculation Board

and her spare time for more than fifty years has largely been
taken up in the Guide movement.)

"To be successful is the desire of all healthy and right-
minded people." So wrote Walter Carroll, who was healthy,
right-minded, and certainly very successful. It was a sentiment
with which Miss Collens heartily agreed and, in looking for a
new secretary, she would naturally have expected in Ida
Carroll the daughter some of the qualities she admired in the
father. There was in fact no financial obligation or expecta-
tion in the appointment of Ida, for Dr Carroll, though a life-
long friend of the school, never received a penny for the services
he gave so readily. On one occasion, when there was a minor
accident at the school and commotion reigned, Ida Carroll
had kept calm and sent out for bandages. Miss Collens had
been pleased at such presence of mind, such common sense.
This was not Ida's only quality, as events of nearly half a
century were to prove. Young and ambitious, she clearly shared
her father's view that "it is a right thing to desire success. The
endeavour to develop the best thing that is in us, to the utmost
of our power, is one of the highest aims of life." She demonstrated the validity of her father's opinion that "there is one
quality without which no great work has ever been, or ever
will be, achieved—the quality of thoroughness".

Ida Carroll set about her task as secretary with enthusiasm
and that desirable quality of thoroughness, responding eagerly
and energetically to the leadership of Miss Collens. Although
she had done well at Manchester High School for Girls, Ida
(who acquired shorthand there) never matriculated. At the
age of fifteen she developed peritonitis and was saved, after a
dramatic journey from a cousin's home in Lymm, Cheshire,
by an operation in a Manchester nursing home. For six
months she had lain gravely ill, in a room on the ground floor
of the Carrolls' home in Didsbury, but, without the
drugs now known to medicine, she had pulled through. It was
due to the careful nursing she received, especially from Elsa,
and an adamant refusal to give up.

CHAPTER FOUR

Growth

To measure up to all that is demanded of him, a man must overestimate his capacities.—Goethe

Within five years the Matthay School had again grown very near to bursting point and it was again necessary for Hilda Collens to seek new premises. The rent for the Deansgate studios was high and further expansion there seemed, economically, out of the question. Miss Collens felt—and it was a view shared by her friends and staff—that Deansgate was not the ideal place for a school of music. Smart shops, offices, and business houses made it a fashionable commercial thoroughfare, but the price was too high for a small private school.

In 1933 Miss Collens was approached by the music firm of Boosey and Hawkes, who had just taken premises at No. 93 Oxford Road, nearly a mile from Deansgate, near All Saints. Jack Howard was their manager and in addition they had appointed Frederick Allen, who had been a B.B.C. announcer, manager of an educational department. Boosey and Hawkes suggested to Miss Collens that a move to Oxford Road by the Matthay would be of mutual benefit. Unfortunately, the accommodation available was insufficient for the growing Matthay and reluctantly Miss Collens prepared to let the matter drop and look elsewhere. She would have just one more try.

An approach was made to the landlords of No. 95, Upsons, a firm of footwear manufacturers, and the result was that the Matthay secured the tenancy of the upper part of No. 95 (which was known as 95A) and also the top floor over Boosey's at No. 93. It was slightly more complicated than the previous moves, because rent had to be paid to both Boosey's and Upsons, but the school now had nine rooms and a concert room for seating 150. In August the Matthay moved in.

Looking at the district today, it is difficult to appreciate the boldness of Miss Collens's decision to move to Oxford Road. In 1934 it was a teeming, bustling district. Churches, cinemas, shops, bakeries, factories, public houses, and thousands of terraced houses and their tenants crowded the district—poor, perhaps, but proud. It was the unofficial centre of a great city. At night the trams would bring young people to the dance halls or the brash new cinemas, or to pursue activities which might have surprised Miss Collens had she known of them. (The crimson wallpaper adorning part of the new premises she ascribed simply to an aberration in taste. Whether she stayed in town late enough on Saturday nights to see Oxford Road at its liveliest is doubtful.)

Redevelopment has removed the overcrowding and the squalor. It has also destroyed the vitality. But forty years ago the difference between Deansgate and the All Saints district was marked. If Deansgate was too expensive and too far out of the way for a music school, was not Oxford Road just that little bit too earthy? Miss Collens, mild and ladylike, was not oblivious to the risk she was running. She was not that unworldly. All along she had been taking calculated risks. This was another.

Entrance to the Matthay's new home was by a dark stairway, but the accommodation was palatial in comparison with the rooms in Deansgate. Boosey's charged a good rent and a fair one, but they allowed Miss Collens to have the use of two fine carpets (remnants of which are still in use to this day) and they installed a display cabinet for their music. Over it they had an electric light, wired to their meter in the shop. The idea was that Matthay students would be able to examine the music there and buy it without leaving the school premises. In practice, the light was rarely used because it was a simple matter for the students to slip down to the shop and buy instruments and music there. The light fitting remains, and it is still wired to a separate meter.

The move was expensive, despite the help of kindly land-lords. Alterations were needed and these were done with the advice of Charles Potter, an architect, and the husband of Isabel Souter, a former student of Miss Collens, who was senior music mistress at Culcheth Hall, Bowdon.

The happy "family" atmosphere survived the changes. Writing of her arrival at the school one bleak January morning, Mildred Oldfield wrote:

> Arrive at Matthay School at 10.25 a.m. and push open little swing door. Amazing noise issues from interior regions. . . . Am greeted by a cheery voice. Another flight of steps and Secretary ushers me into a small cloakroom where a valiant search is made for an empty hook. Am struck by the general hilarity of surging throng, and feel convinced at outset that school must be A Jolly Place.

Her first impressions proved correct, for two months later she noted: "All doubts about wisdom of taking up music now removed owing to joy accruing from course, and friendliness of everybody."

The friendliness of everybody. It is a phrase which recurs with the persistence of a Wagnerian motif throughout the story of Hilda Collens's school. At first, social events simply happened. Now, with the number of students around 170, there was some need for planning. The spirit of spontaneity endured and the students' annual picnic had become another cherished Matthay tradition. Even rain did not dampen the enthusiasm or mar the mood of friendliness. In July 1936 bad weather denied the students full use of the grounds of Lawton Hall, near Congleton, in Cheshire. They did manage to organise a tennis tournament between showers, have their annual game of rounders, and play table tennis. They enjoyed themselves. Hilda Collens and the Present Students' Association—flourishing with Diana Lockhart as secretary and Dorothy Pilling as treasurer—made sure of that.

The staff was much larger and among the London professors who visited the school as examiners, lecturers, or teachers
were Harold Craxton, Clifford Curzon, Dawson Freer and
Frederick Moore. Another was Percy Waller, who must have
been gratified to see how well the frail seedling he had planted
had grown.

Speech and prize days, or what Miss Collens preferred to
call the Distribution of Awards, had become an annual event.
That for 1936 was held on December 8 at the Milton Hall
under the chairmanship of Walter Carroll. The presentations
were made by Frank Roscoe, whose inspection of the school's
training course for teachers several years earlier had led to
its registration.

A month after the annual distribution, on January 8, 1937,
sixty-nine people attended a reunion dinner. Miss Collens
proposed the formation of an association for past students.
It was unanimously agreed upon and Miss Collens was elected
president. Walter Carroll, Macpherson, Moore, and Mrs Moon
became vice-presidents. A committee was formed and Thomas
Cooke became chairman, Doris Euerby secretary, and Ida
Carroll treasurer.

One of the aims of the Old Students' Association was to help
in finding posts for members and to preserve the "family" links.

A direct result of the formation of the O.S.A. was the
publication that summer of a school magazine, edited by
Mary Dunkerley with the help of Mary Bell. The new journal
proudly carried contributions by Macpherson, who wrote of
the importance of having a sense of direction, and Walter
Carroll, who wrote of success. There were also contributions
in verse and prose by students. Pride of place was given to an
article by Miss Collens, which gave a brief account of the
school's progress. She ended with a reference to the move to
Oxford Road:

This change necessitated much expense and outlay, and
anxious times lay ahead; the school had no outside financial

help; it had lived entirely by reason of its work, but already events have proved that the move was a right one and today the school can boast of some two hundred students, the largest number at any one time in its existence.

The educational side of the work has extended in all directions; the staff is now a large one and includes many professors who are musicians of high standing in the country, and whilst any orchestral instrument, besides piano, singing and organ, may be studied, *the Class Music forms as an essential part of the curriculum* as it did in the earliest days of the school, and has greatly increased in scope and importance.

Miss Collens put on record her appreciation of the help and advice of Macpherson, who had inspected the work of the school the previous October, and to Walter Carroll. She ended her message:

The growth of the school educationally and numerically has been highly satisfactory, but throughout this has been made possible by the goodwill and camaraderie which have existed amongst all who have been connected with it; the fine *esprit de corps* which that first little band possessed has been handed on, and to this may largely be attributed any success which the school may claim to have had. Amongst much joy and happiness there have been times when, to the writer, difficulties have seemed almost insuperable but always from behind the clouds has again shone the sun and she has felt that the effort was worth while. That the school may go on from strength to strength is her earnest desire and prayer.

She was pleased with the examination successes. During the previous twelve months twenty L.R.A.M. diplomas had been gained by students. Of these eleven were for the piano and four for aural training class-teaching. Eric Dickinson received an A.T.C.L. diploma for piano (performers). There was a fall in the number of L.R.A.M.s won during the following year. The total was eleven, seven of which were for the piano. Of these seven L.R.A.M.s for piano only one, that awarded to Myra Scott, was for performer. The others were teacher diplomas—a guide to the school's continuing emphasis on the training of teachers.

Although there was a reduction in the number of L.R.A.M. diplomas won that year, it is only fair to record that five other diplomas were awarded to Matthay students, of which four were for elocution, a sign of the success of the new elocution course. May Jepps became a licentiate of Trinity College, London, and Margaret Ashworth, Marion Royle (merit), and Kathleen Warburton licentiates of the Guildhall School.

Examination successes, the inauguration of the Old Students' Association, and publication of the first issue of the magazine were important events, and were just part of the pattern of active life in 1937. In March, Clifford Curzon had spent two days at the school giving master classes in piano-playing to senior students, one of whom recalled that "these lessons were certainly a test of both mental and physical endurance, but they were also a delight". Curzon, whose distinguished teachers had included Matthay, ranged over the early classical period, including Arne, Haydn, Mozart, and early Beethoven, the later classical period, including Beethoven's *Waldstein* sonata and *Emperor* concerto, and the romantic period of Schumann and Schubert. Eileen Chadwick, one of those who attended the master classes, said: "We were all impressed by the intense concentration and attention to significant detail that Mr Curzon devoted to each work. The time spent, though in reality about eight or nine hours, seemed much less."

Another distinguished friend who had visited the school in March was Dr Carroll, who had been obliged to retire in 1934 as Manchester's musical adviser on reaching the age of sixty-five. (His great friend, the distinguished musicologist Percy A.

Scholes, had written at the time[1]: "We have an Archbishop of Canterbury born in 1864 and a Prime Minister born in 1866, but the Musical Adviser to the Manchester Education Committee, born in 1869, is, by Mede-and-Persian law now decreed too old to serve the community. It is, perhaps, an unconscious compliment to the educationist that in his mid-sixties he is always told to go and dig his garden or fish for trout.")

On his retirement, Carroll had said: "I mean to work harder than ever—lecturing, composing, writing, and *living*." He had been doing just that, and his visit to the Manchester branch of the Matthay on March 7 was to give the first of occasional summer-term lectures. He did not lecture about music. He talked to the students about a recent lecture tour he had undertaken in South Wales, where his audiences were mainly unemployed miners. He had been impressed by their wonderful spirit which triumphed over poverty and by their appreciation of culture—especially music.

It was an unusual sort of lecture but, then, Carroll was an unusual man and the Matthay was an unusual school. To Carroll, to Macpherson, to Hilda Collens, music was something more than an esoteric pursuit or recondite hobby. It was part of life, an important part which with the other arts would enrich it. Carroll's missionary work went on and his lecture in March won many converts.

The second lecture of the series was given by an Anglican priest, Miss Collens's friend, the Rev. J. R. H. Moorman,[2] rector of Fallowfield, at whose Sunday school Miss Collens taught each week. Moorman told of his work as a parish priest and the students were probably relieved to find that he had a keen sense of humour. He did not have to cut his cloth to suit his audience.

The lectures by Carroll and Moorman (followed in June by one by Granville Hill of the *Manchester Guardian* on the

---

[1] *The Music Teacher,* June 1934.
[2] Now Bishop of Ripon.

piano and chamber music) were well received at the school. Miss Collens's Christian influence was working quietly, without any suggestion of compulsion. School prayers from the earliest days had been an accepted part of life. The finances were never much better than precarious but there were often little collections for worthy causes and in September 1937 the students decided to "adopt" a boy in a Barnardo home. To do this, they needed to guarantee £35 a year, which seemed a large sum for such a small school to raise. The students offered to guarantee half that sum with the promise of raising as much extra as they could. Most of the full-time students agreed to give one penny a week and Raymond Bertram Egan, a bright and mischievous six-year-old with curly red hair, unexpectedly found himself receiving the attentions of a large, young, and musical family.

The school library was growing, but the additions were not all concerned exclusively with aspects of music. True, it now boasted Schweitzer on Bach and D'Indy on César Franck, but it also possessed H. V. Morton's *In the Steps of St Paul,* E. V. Lucas's *A Wanderer in Florence*, Lytton Strachey's *Eminent Victorians*, and *The Story of My Life* by Helen Keller. This random selection from the stock of the Matthay's library provides a further indication of the school's wide interests.

The staff and students worked hard at their music, too. The school had early earned itself the reputation and the nickname "workhouse", although the "inmates" were there by choice and most of them were thoroughly enjoying the experience. Very often the students gave public performances, of which the most important was the annual orchestral concert. The seventh of these was given at the Houldsworth Hall on March 12, 1937. The main item in the programme conducted by Rees was Beethoven's *Emperor* concerto in which the soloist was Myra Scott. The school choir, by now one of the best in the Manchester area as a result of the inspired training of Gertrude Riall, sang Armstrong Gibbs's setting of

Tennyson's poem, *The Lady of Shalott*. Grainger's *Handel in the Strand*, played by Joan Allott, took the concert out of the rut of conventional programme selection and Haydn's *Military* symphony provided the formal conclusion. It was one of the best concerts the school had given.

On June 5 a special choir, composed of past and present students and trained by Miss Riall, gave a B.B.C. North regional broadcast.

The summer concert at the Milton Hall on July 8 was notable for the "astonishing performance" of a nine-year-old pianist, Hubert Harry, who played pieces by Schumann with "quite unusual poise and charm". A talented violinist of the junior school, Madge Beaumont, aged thirteen, impressed the audience by her beautiful tone in playing a Purcell sonata.

July was kinder for the annual school picnic to Lawton Hall than it had been the year before and the tennis tournament went on without interruption by rain. One student reported: "Play was hardly serious enough to compare favourably with Wimbledon." The school secretary, Ida Carroll, a fine string player, shared the booby prize.

The new school year which started that autumn maintained the pace. The atmosphere of friendship was unimpaired. Collections for the Barnardo boy continued. The awards at the annual distribution at the Milton Hall on December 7 were presented by Dr E. C. S. Dickson, lecturer in acoustics at Manchester University. Walter Carroll again was chairman. The concert which followed, chosen to show the range of the school's work and the talents of some of the students, was typically unstuffy. Eileen Chadwick played Mozart piano music, Marjorie Proudlove played two "fanciful" piano pieces by Pick-Mangiagilli, and a third pianist, Myra Scott, played Brahms. Margaret Carrier, accompanied by Albert Knowles, sang three songs by Peter Warlock, and there were also choral items conducted by Gertrude Riall.

Many of the Matthay's students were juniors who came only once a week. Saturday mornings, when Miss Collens and

her staff gave tuition without pay, were particularly popular.
One junior student, Muriel Christian, gave an account of such
a visit. She said :

> On arriving at the Matthay School at 10 minutes past 10,
> this girl of whom we are speaking goes upstairs to the
> cloakroom. Here she takes off her outdoor clothes and makes
> herself respectable. Not being one of the very young juniors
> she does not have Aural immediately, but goes downstairs
> for Rudiments. For half an hour she has Rudiments in the
> room next door to the library. After this she goes into the
> Concert Room and has Aural for half an hour. If exams
> are near, she has to play scales and pieces.
> When Aural is over, she has 15 minutes to wait before
> her lesson commences. These she spends in talking in the
> tearoom and in eating her lunch. Next she has 40 minutes
> pianoforte lesson. After her lesson she obtains a fresh packet
> of sight-reading from the cupboard in the Library. As she
> has quite a long way to go in order to catch her bus, she
> hurries upstairs to the cloakroom and puts on her hat and
> coat. She reaches home about half past one, after a busy
> and enjoyable morning.

Part-time tuition had developed as an important aspect of
the Matthay's activities. It was provided not only for children
still at school who wished to learn an instrument, but was
also available to adults, including performers, teachers, and
amateurs, who wished to study music, perhaps to gain further
qualifications or to raise their standard of performance and
appreciation. Fees were low and for the staff (most of them
paid little or nothing at all for this voluntary work) it was a
labour of love. Thousands of children benefited by the work
of the part-time department.

On January 7 the Old Students' Association welcomed in
1938 with their second annual dinner and Doris Euerby, the
honorary secretary, reported that "the genial atmosphere we

have grown to expect at all functions connected with Miss Collens and the Matthay School was very evident". The annual students' party on February 8 was held at the school and was so successful that an excuse was found to hold another, this time in fancy dress, at the end of the Easter term.

Musical events included the appearance of a special choir of past and present members of the school at a Tuesday Midday Concert. The choir, conducted by Gertrude Riall, sang Sibelius's *Impromptu*. Myra Scott played Brahms's first piano sonata at the same concert. In March, at the school's orchestral concert at the Houldsworth Hall, Maurice Clare, the newly-appointed professor of the violin, played a Mozart concerto. The symphony was Beethoven's first. William Rees "conducted the orchestra in his usual vital, masterful manner". In May, Clare and students of his ensemble class gave a chamber concert in the school concert room. The main work was Delius's sonata for violin and piano, in which Clare was joined by Albert Knowles.[3]

Summer brought the second issue of the school magazine, with articles by Freer, who gave some practical hints on practising, Dr William Griffiths, who quoted Shelley and O'Shaughnessy in a discussion on the beauty of music, and Dr Annie Warburton, who expanded on the training of taste.

Thomas Cooke, chairman of the the Old Students' Association committee, contributed reviews of four music books. Other items included a message from Miss Collens, who looked ahead three years to the school's twenty-first birthday. She was already considering "what form our celebrations shall take". Three years was a long way ahead, for 1938 was the year of Munich, when so many people hoped that Chamberlain really had achieved peace in their time and that the gathering storm clouds would soon have a silver lining. Twelve months later, however, the school magazine was reflecting the prevailing gloom, although the editorial of July 1939 still held out hope:

---

[3] Later, and now, répétiteur at Covent Garden.

Our third number records steady work and progress, though world events this year have been so momentous that we have wondered at times whether there was a future for the Magazine, for Music, or indeed, for any of us.

So much has been said and written about current events that one would not mention them, but an inspiring truth has been reaffirmed in recent months: Music is a universal language, a common tongue shared and enjoyed by all nationalities.

At the recent London Music Festival the cosmopolitan nature of the audiences has been most noticeable and though many listeners were exiles from their own countries, music was a joy to all.

In our schools, too, refugee children battling with subjects in an unfamiliar tongue have brightened visibly to find that Beethoven is the same in Manchester as in Prague.

With Pope we can say—

> "Music the fiercest grief can charm
> And fate's severest rage disarm."

For the moment, the school could concentrate on celebrating the twenty-first anniversary of the holiday course for teachers, founded in 1919 by Mildred Esplin. In 1920, just before the second annual course began, she became ill and sent all the letters, cheques, and forms to Miss Collens, with a covering note: "I am in bed with a bad quinsy; please will you take over the entire management of the 'course' . . . will you meet Mr Ernest Read at the Midland Hotel at 11 a.m., and look out for Mr Stewart Macpherson, who will arrive later?" Hilda Collens did as she was asked. She recalled: "My heart banged with pleasurable excitement. Suffice it to say that the week proved to be one of the happiest of my life." For the next few years the two young women collaborated in running the annual course and, as we have seen, in founding the Manchester branch of the Matthay.

The holiday course came of age in July 1939, and the week

of celebrations began with a gathering of friends at St Ann's Parish Church, for a thanksgiving service. Moorman gave the address, and the lesson was read by Dr Carroll. The school choir, conducted by Gertrude Riall, led the hymns and sang Schubert's setting of the Twenty-third Psalm. The organist was Albert Knowles. The service over, the congregation, augmented by members of the Old Students' Association in Manchester for their summer meeting, then walked over to the Milton Hall for tea, at which the guest of honour was Macpherson, who had been the sole lecturer at the first holiday course. Then, with the informalities and presentations completed, Macpherson opened the course with a lecture on the music of Hadyn.

An innovation at the twenty-first course was the series of master classes given by Clifford Curzon. Walter Carroll's lecture dealt with voice training. "With the assistance of ten small boys who gave illustrations with the most superb nonchalance, he managed to pack into the short space of an hour an incredible amount of useful information, interspersed with some hilarity." Dorothy Pilling, an active member of the magazine committee, continued her report: "Dr Carroll is at his best with boys; his benevolent amusement at their mistakes never irritates them; his fund of humorous anecdotes diverts them, and his constant encouragement spurs them to further efforts." Another popular lecturer was Hilda Collens, organiser of the course. "Everyone obviously appreciated particularly the practical value of her lecture, and, judging, by the voluminous notes taken, members gleaned many ideas which they were determined to use in their own work at the earliest opportunity."

It was a very happy week. The musicians dispersed to their homes in various parts of Britain, looking forward to the twenty-second holiday course next July. It never took place. A month after the joyous celebrations Britain was at war.

Tobias Matthay

Stewart Macpherson

Ernest Read

Walter Carroll

CHAPTER FIVE

War Efforts

Hope is generally a wrong guide, though it is very good company by the way.
—George Savile, Marquis of Halifax

One of the first of the Matthay "family" to come face to face with the reality of war was Helen Wright. She was on the liner *Athenia* that September, returning to a teaching post in Canada. The *Athenia* was torpedoed and she was one of the survivors. But for the moment the Matthay, like the rest of Britain, could hope that the war would soon be over, attend to the blackout, and maintain a cheery optimism. The school had recently been encouraged by several successes: Dorothy Yates, who had been trained in the junior school, had won Manchester education committee's annual music scholarship and had taken up studies in the senior section; John Davies, a fine pianist and the first full-time male student at the school, had taken part in Hallé concerts during the winter of 1939–40; and during the same winter Tuesday Midday Concerts were given by Dorothy Pilling, Albert Knowles, and Davies.

Old students were increasingly successful in getting appointments including, in that first year of war, teaching posts at Kendal, Stafford, Bowdon, Glossop, Sale, Folkestone, and Dewsbury, and at Manchester High School for Girls and Notre Dame High School, Manchester.

John Pye, a member of the junior school, obtained 142 marks out of a possible 150 in the Associated Board final grade examinations held in July 1939, winning the gold medal for the highest number of marks gained in this grade in the British Isles. Another junior, Archie Carver, won an exhibition of £40 a year to Rossall School, mainly because of his musical ability.

But 1940 was to bring "sombre tints to the bright picture of the school's progress". Because of evacuation of many children to country areas, there was a fall in the number of students. And early in the year Miss Collens went down with shingles. It was a long and trying illness. She was forbidden all work for several months and went to recuperate at Penrhyn Bay before returning to her home at 30B Palatine Road, Withington. The school carried on although, as Mary Dunkerley observed, "it seemed a strange place without her stimulating presence". In March, John Davies died and a promising career was snuffed out. Davies was only thirty but he had, as already mentioned, realised his ambition of playing with the Hallé, and he had drawn full houses at the two midday concerts he had given. He had a cheerful personality and he was a good musician, as Dr Carroll had realised when, as Manchester's music adviser, he had discovered Davies playing the accompaniment for the choral class at Princess Road School. Carroll told Sir Hamilton Harty, who was equally impressed by Davies's outstanding qualities as a musician. Davies, educated at Central High School (where he matriculated), studied at the Matthay after winning Manchester education committee's music scholarship in 1927. After further study in Germany he embarked upon a concert career. His death after a long illness was a sad blow to his friends at the Matthay, where he was remembered for his vitality and gaiety.

The Matthay's contribution to the war effort was not confined to making music, although the war years were remarkable for attendances at concerts. "House full" notices were often seen at Hallé concerts and there was similar enthusiasm at most musical events—an enthusiasm which, the 1942 school magazine hoped, would surely "go forward into that 'brave new world' that we all hope lies ahead".

Meanwhile, there were jobs to be done, a war to be won, before the brave new world could become anything more than a dream. Many old students were serving in the armed forces, of course, but some were in less likely occupations. One was doing laundry work, perhaps listening with a more than ordinarily appreciative ear to the radio programme "Workers' Playtime". Another "old girl" was doing a man's work inspecting factories. Emily Hector, temporarily forsaking Beethoven, became a milk-van driver for Buxton Co-op. Molly Hibbert, who until 1941 had been a member of the Old Students' Association committee, became (as if to show her versatility) an assistant horticulture supervisor.

For those intrigued readers of the school magazine in July 1943, Molly Hibbert explained how she was helping 500 schoolchildren at Ashton-under-Lyne, Lancashire, to "dig for victory" by taking gardening as a school subject.

Miss Hibbert wrote: "Some of the 12-plus scholars work at their own allotments at their own schools, and for these we allocate seeds, raise plants for bedding out, and offer advice to the school staff if they require it; but the bulk of the children work directly under the Garden Centre Staff at four main centres. . . . In summertime it is barely an exaggeration to say we work from dawn to dark." They were getting "quite good results in food production" and there was also "a satisfying feeling not only in the knowledge that one is doing work of national importance, but in the daily contact with 'the good earth' ".

It was a long way from Scarlatti and exercises in counterpoint to raising tomatoes in the unlikely climate of Ashton-under-Lyne, but the war saw millions of people doing unusual things. Several other old students found themselves nearer "the good earth" as members of the Women's Land Army.

Hilda Collens received warm letters of greeting from old students scattered "somewhere in England" and throughout the world. She was greatly comforted by those from men and women serving in the forces. She told the school, at the annual distribution of awards held at the Lower Albert Hall on February 27, 1942 : "It is a great joy to receive letters from them and to hear how, in the midst of their army life, they are managing to snatch every possible chance of music making and music hearing. We are living in a mechanical age, but it is up to those of us who love Art to see that it shall never die."

George Fisher was one old student now on active service in the army. Instead of a field-marshal's baton in his knapsack, he packed several scores, including those of *Falstaff*, César Franck's Symphony in D minor, Beethoven's Opus 111 piano sonata, and Schubert's posthumous B flat sonata. These he carried with him to the trenches "to occupy his spare minutes". [After the war he returned to the school to learn the clarinet.]

Diana Lockhart, a talented pianist, volunteered for overseas service with the Y.M.C.A. and drove a mobile canteen through France in 1944. Her war service did not end with driving the canteen and helping to feed the invading Allied troops. She would, a member of her party wrote home to the school, "be useful on the entertainment side, for some of the canteens have drop sides which are used as platforms for concert work". So Diana Lockhart, far removed from the cosy formality of a concert hall, gave recitals from the sides of mobile canteens!

Others gave concerts to tired factory workers, or, by raising large sums of money by giving recitals, were able to give generous help to prisoners of war. Dr Carroll, never slow to help, had been eager to organise series of concerts for the Forces and these, presented at the Manchester Y.M.C.A., were given by students of the school. His daughter Ida, after finding the hours of a part-time telephonist inconvenient, became a diligent air-raid warden in the Didsbury and Withington districts of the city.

The Matthay and everyone connected with it seemed to be doing their bit to win the war, even to the extent of bringing many pounds of soap to a bring-and-buy sale. The soap was for Mrs Churchill's "Aid to Russia" Fund.

The school escaped a direct hit in the blitz on Manchester just before Christmas 1940, although the Royal Manchester College of Music, just over half a mile away, suffered considerable damage. But two neighbouring churches were destroyed and every window in the Matthay School was smashed.

First thing next morning Ida Carroll went down into the shop of Boosey and Hawkes and found a handyman on Boosey and Hawkes business. She told him about the school's windows, impressed upon him that something had to be done immediately, and quickly requisitioned his services.

Glass was not available, so together they set off for Pauldens' store, then nearby at All Saints. There they bought rolls of plain brown linoleum which, time being of the essence, they carried through All Saints back to the school. Although she was the school secretary Miss Carroll, then as now, was not one to stand and wait for things to happen.

Miss Carroll then enlisted another man from Boosey and Hawkes, this one a joiner. The manager of the shop had by this time heard of the loss of his first man. "I believe you've got one of my men working for you," he said to her. "No," she replied, "I've got two." Very soon, a third man—the manager—was doing all he could to help the school to get back to normal.

The linoleum was used to seal the windows (thereby blacking out the school) and the partitions which had been blown in were pushed back into place. Within two hours the school was back in business.

The school had "been exhorted to carry on as normally as possible in these troubled times", and it did so, although by electric lamplight. The twenty-first anniversary was duly celebrated in June 1941 with three concerts at the Lower Albert Hall, the second raising £14 18s. 6d. towards the scholarship fund which the Old Students' Association at the suggestion of Doris Fox had set up to mark the school's coming-of-age. Dr Carroll, who in 1941 was appointed honorary music adviser, was a frequent lecturer. Professor T. H. Pear also lectured at the school and wrote for the magazine. The annual picnic was a casualty, but other social events, such as theatre outings, were organised.

One such theatre outing was to an afternoon performance of *La Traviata* given by the Vic-Wells company at Stockport.

Dorothy Pilling, recording the visit in 1941, wrote prophetically: "We must certainly count it one of the few advantages of the war that a good London company should perform so far from its headquarters, and we hope this state of affairs will continue long after these days of stress have become but a horrid memory."

The annual school parties continued in spite of rationing. This "indefatigable function", as it was proudly termed, was (and is) a happy event. "Had Herr Hitler been privileged to see the avalanche of delicious food with which we were confronted . . . he would have surrendered at once, overcome with despair and rage at our triumph over his 'counter blockade'! Though the party ended much earlier than usual it made up in quality what it lacked in quantity."

Academically, the school survived the upheavals. Diplomas awarded to students during the year ended July 1940 numbered ten, including an F.R.C.O. to George Fisher (who was to continue his studies in the trenches) and an L.R.A.M. diploma in elocution to Adelaide Trainor, who was later to do sterling work with the school drama classes. Five L.R.A.M.s went to pianists and there were four in aural training. Twenty-three pianists were awarded Associated Board certificates in various grades: the successful candidates included John Pye, whose gold medal has already been mentioned, and Vincent Billington, who took the elementary grade with distinction.

Twelve months later, the emphasis was still on pianists, but among the thirteen diplomas in music, one was for the violin (to William Millne) and one was for voice culture (to Harry O'Brien). Of the seventeen Associated Board certificates gained, two went to violinists, one to a singer, and the remaining fourteen to pianists, including an advanced grade with distinction to Greta Jackson, a pupil of Doris Euerby. Greta Jackson also won the Associated Board gold medal for the highest marks in the United Kingdom in the Grade VII examinations.

The developing interest in strings was reflected the following year when, of the twenty-seven Associated Board certificates awarded, seven went to string players.

The numbers of examination successes are given for those early war years to allow a comparison with the results being achieved despite wartime difficulties. By July 1945 the senior school could report one Mus.B., nine L.R.A.M.s (including that to Herbert Winterbottom, for the piano), one A.R.C.M., and twenty-three Associated Board certificates. The junior school students collected fifty-seven Associated Board certificates.

Although a school of music cannot be judged on examination successes alone, the numbers suggest a dramatic growth in the school's activities in the short space of five years. The rate of expansion was to continue in the succeeding years of peace.

CHAPTER SIX

The Northern School

A good name is rather to be chosen than great riches.
—Proverbs

The Manchester branch of the Matthay School celebrated its twenty-first birthday in 1941. It was a time to look back with pride and to look forward with hope. In her report to the school at the annual distribution of awards in February 1942, Miss Collens recalled the progress which had been made over the years. She said:

> Now we have nearly 200 students, good premises, and a staff of thirty highly-trained professors. In consequence we are able to offer a complete training in its various branches. We have a large junior school and a flourishing Old Students' Association, which is responsible for the school magazine. We have a recognised course of training for teachers, our own orchestra, choir, and chamber music classes. We support a child in Dr Barnardo's Homes and during last year we collected more than £30 for other objects. We are conscious of having made many mistakes, but we are happy to feel that today we hold a secure place and contribute in no small way to the musical life of the city and district. Our former students hold important positions in various parts of the kingdom and, within a few miles' radius of this hall [the Lower Albert Hall] no less than twenty-four secondary schools draw their music staff from them. If the number of scholars in these schools averaged only 350—and it is probably higher—it would mean that we were responsible for the musical training of 8,400 children, and this estimate does not include many elementary and some private schools.

Miss Collens urged the present students to hand on their heritage of "hard work combined with happy fellowship and mutual confidence" to the next generation of students "so that at the end of another twenty-one years the school may stand with its roots still more firmly planted".

Until now the school had been a strictly private enterprise. This, as Miss Collens observed, had given it "a certain personality which might otherwise not have existed". The individuality of which Miss Collens was so justly proud was certainly a product of private, rather than institutional enterprise, and the Matthay had been prospering. But the war had brought many uncertainties and there were constant financial pressures to dog such a private and highly individualistic artistic organisation.

For some time Miss Collens had been concerned for the future stability of the school. In twenty-one years the Matthay had expanded enormously, but so had the problems. Furthermore, as she remarked: "A school is not easy to steer successfully in war-time." She was voicing publicly the fears which had been troubling her privately for some years. She had thought long and deeply about the problem. War added the element of urgency to her deliberations. Young men and women were joining the armed forces, children were being evacuated to safer parts of the country, and enrolments at the Matthay had fallen sharply.

There were those who still suspected that Miss Collens was running the school for considerable financial gain. The fact was that she lived frugally and put everything she earned back into the school. When she died she left very little apart from a house and her pianos. Doris Euerby, one of the original nine students, who joined the staff in 1923, says that in those early years she received no salary, but the fees she received for tuition amounted to the princely sum of £25 a term! Clearly there was not much money for salaries. What seems to have kept the staff was their dedication to the work of the school. One staff member recalls that she gave up a much better paid teaching job to return to the school. That was true of many others. "So long as we knew that we had enough to buy our next meal, we didn't worry."

After much heart-searching, Hilda Collens decided that a radical change would be in the best interests of the school. Instead of being a purely private concern, it would be put "on a public basis". Early in 1942 Miss Collens instructed her solicitors to begin the formalities for a change in the school's constitution.

Not everyone was convinced that the change would be for the better. Some feared that the school would lose its individuality, its atmosphere of friendship. There were some, naturally, who opposed change simply because it was change. Hilda Collens had the vision of a stronger school and she believed the change to be necessary. She also understood the misgivings, for she herself had shared them. Having overcome them, she applied herself to the task with enthusiasm. She took the school and the old students into her confidence.

In a message she wrote: "Some of you may feel a pang of regret, but I hope and believe that you will think it a right step to take." She also gave the assurance: "So long as I am Principal the actual conduct of the school will not be changed."

In 1943, when the formalities were nearly complete, she wrote:

The change will mean that the school will have the advantage of the help and co-operation of a few distinguished ladies and gentlemen who have kindly promised to act as a Council, so that it will be able to apply for many benefits which are withheld from private schools, and that its life will become more permanent.

The parting of the ways is always a little difficult, but in the past I have received a great deal of help from my old students, and now I ask for still more. I want the school, even in these difficult days, to go on from strength to strength, so that we may all continue to be proud of it and that it may be worthy of our pride and devotion.

The Matthay School, Manchester branch, formally became a public institution in the autumn of 1943, taking the name "The Northern School of Music". The memorandum and articles of association forming a company "limited by guarantee and not having a share capital" were signed by Leslie A. Boosey, chairman of Boosey and Hawkes Ltd; Clifford Curzon; W. F. S. Holmes, who was the secretary of the Northern Universities Joint Matriculation Board; J. W. Johnson, a banker, of Stockport; Mildred Moon (*née* Esplin), then a magistrate living in Leicester Road, Hale; and Frederick Moore and Ernest Read, professors at the Royal Academy of Music.

The certificate of incorporation, omitting the word "limited", was signed by P. Eke, Assistant Registrar of Companies, at Llandudno, on September 15, 1943.

The Northern was now a non-profit-distributing body and there was provision for a council of management of no fewer than six members and no more than fifteen.

The original council comprised all the signatories of the articles of association. In addition, Freer, professor of the Royal College of Music, and Dr Francis H. S. Curd, a research chemist and a nephew of Miss Collens, were founder members. Holmes, whom Miss Collens had met at the Carrolls' home in Didsbury, accepted an invitation to become the chairman.

The council's first meeting began at noon on November 2, 1943, at 76 Cross Street, Manchester—the school's registered office. Holmes was in the chair. Other council members present were Johnson, Curd, and Mrs Moon. It was a fairly brief and formal meeting. Roger Carter, of Carter, Chaloner, and Kearns, the firm which had handled financial and other aspects of the negotiations, produced the certificate of incorporation. Formally, the agreement under which the business formerly carried on by Miss Collens had become the Manchester branch of the Matthay School of Music was assigned to the association and the new company seal affixed.

The minutes of that historic meeting were recorded in a large new minute-book. They were entered then, as they have been ever since, in the neat handwriting of the new company secretary. The council had appointed Ida Carroll.

CHAPTER SEVEN

Peace

Better a lean peace than a fat victory.
—Seventeenth-century English proverb

Although 1945 brought peace, it also brought problems for
the Northern. Men returning from the forces, wishing to
continue their music studies or train as music teachers, sought
admission to the Northern's courses. The editorial of the school
magazine published that July stated: "Now we must think
about housing our school in a building worthy of its name."
It went on:

> We have always known, and the war has emphasised this
> cruelly, that buildings in themselves make neither homes
> nor schools. Bombing, which has sent families and institu-
> tions from under their own roofs to many strange places,
> has failed in the main to alter the spirit which is the essential
> feature of home and institutional life.
>
> Those of the Old Students who have followed the School
> from Hime and Addison's to the Tudor Galleries, and from
> 260 Deansgate to its present home, know that though each
> place has been very different from the others, the spirit of
> the school has never changed.

This was the earnest preamble to an urgent appeal. The
sum of £25,000 was needed "to provide a building that would
be really adequate". The extension fund was launched as the
school celebrated its twenty-fifth anniversary.

As part of the celebrations, and also as a way of getting
the extension fund off to a good start, five concerts were given
at the Houldsworth Hall in June and July. Students, former
students, and friends, were urged to "support these efforts as

61

never before for the good of the cause. We need and want a fine building". They responded generously. The first concert, given by students, was of piano music by romantic or "modern" composers. The second concert was also of piano music, this time played by old students. Composers represented included Mozart, Grieg, Franck, Brahms, Albeniz, Scriabin, and Ireland. The third concert, on June 13, was given by the Junior School and, apart from piano works, included pieces for the violin, and extracts from Daviot's *Richard of Bordeaux* and Goldsmith's *She Stoops to Conquer,* which were given by members of the junior school's elocution section. The fourth concert, on July 13, was given with the Manchester Women's String Orchestra, and the fifth and final concert on July 27 was a representative miscellany. This included much vocal work. The school choir, conducted by Ernest Read, sang part-songs and a setting by Hubert Harry of a poem from Housman's *A Shropshire Lad.* Proceeds of these concerts were shared between the extension fund, and those for the Barnardo boy and the Old Students' Bursary.

The annual holiday course, which followed immediately, added a small contribution to the extension fund as well as providing stimulating lectures by Curzon, Freer, Read, Annie Warburton, Cyril Winn, and Miss Collens. Social events were not neglected and old students seemed to have enjoyed the folk dancing session directed by Molly Hibbert.

Further concerts in aid of the extension fund were organised when the school reassembled for its new academic year that autumn. Among those who took part were the pianist Hubert Harry and Reginald Stead, one of the school's professors of violin, who in 1945 had been appointed leader of the B.B.C. Northern Orchestra.

It was certainly a strenuous winter, raising money for the extension while carrying on the normal work of the school. The acquisition of premises at 91 Oxford Road and the consequent need for several hundred pounds much earlier than expected added to Miss Collens's problems. At the beginning of December the Christmas fair was held, and it was enlivened by the engagement—allegedly "at great expense"— of a scratch orchestra rejoicing under the name "All Saints Philharmonic". Irene Wilde recorded: "Many well-known faces were observed, whose owners played strange instruments with great skill and agility. Among these we feel that we should mention Miss Collens, whose masterly passages on the tea-tray left us slightly awed." The members might have pressing financial worries, but they could still let their hair down and enjoy themselves.

The death at the age of eighty-seven of Matthay later that month cast some gloom over the Christmas festivities, but the social at the Plaza ballroom on January 5, 1946, went on as planned. The evening "was spent in team games and dancing" in a private suite hired for the occasion.

In the past two years, the staff had been augmented to deal with the heavy demands on the school's facilities. Full-time appointments included Dorothy Pilling, and she was followed by Eileen Chadwick, Irene Wilde, and by Sydney Errington (viola), Clifford Knowles (violin), P. Rider (horn), William Hardwick and Douglas Steele (organ), and Ellis Keeler (singing), who replaced Freer.

Even with an increase in staff, the post-war influx of students, many of them men on ex-service grants, meant a very busy week. Pay was poor, but the staff worked at least twelve hours every day of the week from Monday to Friday. On Saturdays their labour of love ended comparatively early, at 5 p.m.

Various administrative changes were made during these years. Those who had joined the school's council of management included Dr Walter Williams, Dr J. C. Withers, the Rev. Arthur White, and Mrs Crosland. Ill health had forced the resignation in 1945 of Holmes, the first chairman, and Mrs Moon had become deputy chairman.

Ida Carroll was still the school secretary and exercised a typewriter keyboard in a tiny office about eight feet long and four feet wide. Outside was a small counter from which she dispensed prospectuses. Next to the office was an even smaller room where she gave music lessons. At least when work on extensions finally gathered momentum in 1946 there was a much needed gain in office and studio space. (The counter, for sentimental reasons, was allowed to survive these and subsequent alterations.) In 1946 Miss Carroll's burden was lightened by the appointment of Geoffrey Griffiths to the new post of bursar. Until that time Miss Carroll had done all the administrative work, with occasional secretarial help from Mary Farquharson, Mary Thorpe, Dorothy McLoughlin, Margaret Hughes, and others (Pamela Stones became the school secretary in March 1960).

Griffiths had worked in the travel agency where Dr Carroll used to buy his railway tickets for his frequent visits to London. Carroll, discovering that the young man was interested in singing, enlisted Griffiths for his choir at Birch Church. So began "Griff's" association with Dr Carroll and his family and with the work of Hilda Collens and the Northern School. After war service in the Royal Air Force, Griffiths returned to travel agency work in Manchester. His main interest, however, was in music and musicians, and when he was offered the opportunity of a job at the Northern he accepted readily.

The annual picnic in July 1946 took the form of a ramble round Hayfield. It rained most of the day and few turned up. Those who did had several debates on what form the celebrations should take and they decided to visit the open-air swimming baths—which they did, only to find the baths empty, one of the few dry spots in a very damp Derbyshire.

During the summer, old students living in and around London decided to form a branch of the O.S.A. and in September, Miss Collens and Miss Carroll travelled down for the inaugural meeting at the Westway Hotel. Within a few months Milicent Bourne (formerly Webster) the branch's first honorary secretary, was reporting a membership of twenty-three.

Otello by the Choir with the Hallé Orchestra

Among items discussed at those first meetings of the London branch was a problem shared by many of the Northern's old students. This was the question of their teaching status. After the war Miss Collens received many inquiries from old students. Did the training at the Northern and the L.R.A.M. qualification entitle them to the rank of "qualified teacher"? Miss Collens had replied: "The position is a strange one; the 1945 Burnham report only mentions music teachers who hold a graduate qualification; for all others, application to the Ministry [of Education] must be made by the authorities in whose schools they teach."

In July 1946, Miss Collens had been able to assure old students that

. . . every student from this school for whom such application has been made has been given the status and the salary of a qualified teacher. Answers to the applications are often delayed a long time, but when the question is settled, it is retrospective and the teacher receives a cheque for all the money which has been missed in the past.

Miss Collens believed that "before very long" the matter would be "put on a more satisfactory basis", for it was in the summer of 1946 that the Ministry sought the Northern's co-operation in the training of teachers. Miss Collens, willingly giving such co-operation, saw it as "a glorious opportunity to spread still wider our ideals in regard to the teaching of music". More important, it would "give our school a position in the country which cannot be disputed". Miss Collens, who was well aware of the uninformed but often hurtful criticisms made of the school, especially in its early years of alleged commercialism, wanted the Northern to be in an unassailable position. The Northern, a comparative newcomer to the confined little world of music academies, lacked the glamour of the older institutions. To London ears, even the name, the Northern School of Music, was aggressively provincial, redolent of some remote windswept wastelands scarred by the Industrial

E

Revolution. The chance of working with the Ministry of Education in training teachers might indeed put the Northern in an indisputable position. The opportunity was seized.

If Miss Collens thought that this co-operation would help to resolve the recurring problem of recognition for old students "before very long", then she was wrong. The mills of ministries grind slowly and, however much Miss Collens might refer old students to the relevant paragraphs in Ministry of Education circulars, the nagging doubts were to be felt by old students and local authorities for a few more years.

Answering old students' queries on this and other matters added to Miss Collens's burden, but it was additional work which she undertook happily, for she liked to think of all the students, past and present, as part of her "family". The growth of Old Students' Association and its informal "appointments bureau" was increasing the Northern's information about the availability of jobs. This efficient intelligence network, headed by Miss Collens, enabled many old students to find work either as teachers or performers. It involved Miss Collens in much travel and correspondence, in which she was given untiring help by Miss Carroll. The work was done without fuss or undue publicity, and it was done willingly, because it was yet another glorious opportunity to spread the Northern's ideals. For Miss Collens and her staff, however, the most rewarding part of this work was the satisfaction of helping their students.

There were many things to occupy Miss Collens's attention, of which the most pressing was the work on the extensions. Matthay had died, and though to many of the younger staff he was remembered as an elderly, curious man with white hair protruding from a smoking-cap, Miss Collens had felt his loss deeply. He had given his name to the school and when the name was changed he had generously agreed to become the Northern's president. (He was succeeded as president by his pupil, Myra Hess.)

Finance was always a worry to Miss Collens. The school was almost completely dependent upon the fees of the students and upon the generous enthusiasm of the staff, who worked long hours for very little pay. They respected Miss Collens and liked the atmosphere she had created at the Northern. The increase in the number of students, while gratifying, put extra strains on Miss Collens, the small administrative staff, and also on the premises and finances. But the large number of male students meant that a combined choir, including tenors and basses, could now be formed, and the drama department was blossoming under the direction of Adelaide Trainor.

Miss Trainor had begun her association with the department in 1938 and became director of the course in 1942 in succession to Dorothy Robinson. At the end of the war the department had only one full-time student and the classes were made up by students who wished to go on into opera or by those who wanted to improve their speech. Like the rest of the Northern School, the department grew quickly and by February 1946 was giving one-act plays at the Institute of Adult Education in Lower Mosley Street. On their return visit, on May 22, 1947, members of the drama class gave two one-act plays. The school magazine reported :

In *At the Hawk's Well*, by W. B. Yeats, they displayed their appreciation of the strange beauty of his lyric verse and showed considerable resource in costume and movement in this fantastic piece. Enid Openshaw in particular showed a developing sense of characterisation in the part of the Old Man. Dulac's very effective incidental music, given by two students of the school, Margaret Moore (oboe) and Lydia Richards (harp), was an invaluable aid to the atmosphere of the play.

The second play, *End and Beginning*, by Masefield, deals with the last hours of Mary Queen of Scots, immediately before her execution. Edith Whiteside, as the ill-fated queen, gave a sensitive performance, the more moving on account of its restraint and dignity; she received responsive support from Audrey Latham as one of her ladies. Brian Evans, a member of the Junior School, gave a well-poised and debonair performance as a noble. . . .

By the summer of 1947 the extensions and alterations were at last nearing completion, the school's newly formed branch of the Student Christian Movement had twenty active members, and the school's Barnardo boy, Raymond Egan, was now aged thirteen and making steady progress at Watt's Naval Training School at Elmham, Norfolk. He was third in a class of thirty-six and was also doing well in athletics, swimming and cricket. Summer concerts at the Houldsworth Hall included two piano recitals by senior students and a concert by the junior school in which the young pianist Vincent Billington played the first movement of a Haydn concerto with the junior school orchestra conducted by Ida Carroll. The main annual summer concert on July 24 featured much chamber music and "a robust performance" of numbers from Bach's *Peasant Cantata*. Among lecturers at the holiday course held a few days later were Curzon and his wife, the American-born harpischordist Lucille Wallace, Keeler, and Dr Annie Warburton.

By September the extensions were completed at last, several months later than Miss Collens had expected, and the school was able to spread into No. 91 Oxford Road and take advantage. Miss Collens was able to report to old students that the school now had "quite a different appearance".

She wrote:

You entered by another door and found the offices and waiting rooms on the ground floor; if you turned to the office on the right, you would be greeted by our kindly Bursar, Mr Griffiths, whose coming has added a great deal to the well-being of the school. In the office on the left Miss Ida Carroll still holds sway, and without her the school would be quite incomplete. Upstairs you would find many studios but many people whom you would recognise, amongst them Miss Doris Euerby and Miss Beatrice Rollins, who do so much for the School. In the basement you would doubtless discover the canteen, the boon to many tea-drinkers, including myself!

It was now possible for 140 students to gather on Friday mornings for the appreciation class, aural practice, and choir. The choir was divided into "A" and "B" sections. The "A" section, with S.A.T.B. voices, was conducted by Miss Riall, the "B" section by Irene Wilde. Classes for stringed instruments were started and, "thanks to the energy and enterprise of Miss Ida Carroll", the school could boast of three orchestras which on Friday afternoons tackled music ranging from "simple Bach suites to symphonies and concertos". There were now not only string-players but wind-players, too, and also two harpists and a timpanist. The recent acquisition of kettledrums, a side-drum, a glockenspiel and cymbals had not been in vain. The school's singing section was reported to be "very strong" and piano studies were flourishing.

The school's expanding activities were reflected in the variety offered at various public concerts. The annual distribution of awards, held on January 30, 1948, was notable for the presence of the Lord Mayor of Manchester, Alderman Miss (later Dame) Mary Kingsmill Jones, who presented the awards. Other events during the school year included an oboe recital by Evelyn Rothwell, wife of the Hallé conductor, John Barbirolli. She was accompanied by Rayson Whalley, whom Barbirolli chose the following season to become the Hallé's permanent pianist. Charles Taylor, of the B.B.C. Northern Orchestra and leader of the Taylor String Quartet, joined the staff to teach the violin and take classes in string quartet and sonata playing. The drama department chose Cyril Campion's thriller, *Ladies in Waiting*, and, we are told, "the students as a whole acquitted themselves well". Even if it could not be "ranked as a first-class play", it did offer "good entertainment".

The school year ended, traditionally, with the holiday course which was opened by the soprano Isobel Baillie, accompanied by Whalley. The Curzons again gave master classes on piano and harpsichord works and other lectures were given by Keeler and Dr Warburton. Raymond Egan, having passed his examinations, enlisted in the Royal Navy as "Boy, 2nd Class" and the school adopted nine-year-old Raymond Goddard, then at a Barnardo home at Derby. Pauline Tinsley, who succeeded Mary Bell as honorary secretary of this charitable enterprise, reported him to be a "happy and real boy, enjoying life to the full, and fond of all games". The Meccano set, which was among the gifts the Northern sent him for Christmas, was a particularly happy choice for such a real boy.

Nineteen-forty-eight was another year of growth. A fund to raise the £2,000 needed to create a permanent scholarship had been established, and within six months £500 had been raised. The Old Students' Association bursary fund was still active raising money and helping students. Collections for the Barnardo boy fund were made regularly. Private enterprise was clearly hard-pressed, but the work of the school went on as happily as ever, and Miss Collens's faith served as an inspiration and an incentive.

It was rewarded by the good news from the Ministry of Education that a grant of £250 would be made to the Northern by the local education authority, Manchester. It was a small sum, but the school's council recognised its significance and went ahead with plans to begin a pension fund. It was at this time also that the council took the first steps towards the creation of a Northern School of Music diploma. The increase in the school's activities was quickly followed by several appointments to the staff, including Vere Hardy (trombone), and four B.B.C. Northern Orchestra players, Norman Mansell (viola), Alan Morton (cello), Bernard O'Keefe (oboe), and Cecil Kidd (trumpet).

The school magazine published that long hot summer was the twelfth annual issue. Mary Lockley (formerly Dunkerley), who had edited the magazine since the first publication in 1937, resigned because of growing personal commitments and in her valedictory editorial there was, understandably, more than just a hint of nostalgia:

> How many remember the old Friday mornings when the walls in the Deansgate building then housing the school seemed likely to burst, when to find a corner to eat one's home-packed lunch after Appreciation class was a major problem and to find a peg for one's coat an impossibility? Those old students should view now the extensions to the present premises with their pleasant rooms and canteen.
>
> It has been a constant source of wonder to outsiders that the school has grown to its present size and standing from such a modest beginning and without financial aid. What they have failed to realise is the power of enthusiasm, loyalty, and love. Those who have helped in the building know what an amount of work has been done by staff and students for the sheer love of the subject and with no thought of pecuniary reward.
>
> This enthusiasm and selfishness is infectious and has passed from one generation to another with cumulative effect, and though numbers have increased and contacts widened, there has been no lessening of the loyalty to the school shown by its members. In these qualities perhaps lie the roots from which so much has sprung.

Such were the sentiments which the Northern created and nourished, and they were shared by Mrs Lockley's successor as editor, Dorothy Pilling, who with Ida Carroll and Mrs Lockley had been the triumvirate responsible for the magazine.

The Principal's annual message to her old students, contained in that issue, gave indications of her strong religious feelings. Commenting on the death of Madge Beaumont in December 1947, at the age of twenty-three, Miss Collens was moved to write:

I cannot close this letter without expressing my own
feeling in regard to her. Madge was one of the best students
that we ever had, her violin playing gave me more enjoyment
than that of many better-known artistes, but above her
musical gifts she had a fine character and behind that quiet
manner there was real grit and determination. We all sorrow
for her loss but I feel sure that she is now finding some
higher use for those gifts with which she was so liberally
endowed and which she used to the full.

She noted that Madge's parents were lonely and urged anyone
who knew Madge Beaumont to visit them or to write.

In 1948 there were two more deaths. Holmes died in July
and in reporting his passing "to the higher life", Miss Collens
said that "his wisdom and kindness were invaluable during
the period when the management of the school was changed".
In November, Curd, another school council member, was
among five victims when two trains crashed in dense fog on
Stockport viaduct. Holmes and Curd were remembered gratefully by Miss Collens for "the many times in which they put
their personal convenience on one side in order to serve the
school".

The fog in which Curd was fatally injured was one of the
worst in the Manchester area for years. That night Northern
School musicians gave a recital at the Oxford Hall. The
audience comprised only thirty stalwarts who had found their
way through the fog, but they arrived at the hall before the
soprano, Pauline McCormick. The recital began with items
by the pianist, Mary Robinson. Joy Jung, accompanied by
Rayson Whalley, sang while the audience awaited the arrival
of Miss McCormick. After struggling through the fog, she
arrived an hour late. November 30, 1948, was an unhappy
night for the Northern.

CHAPTER EIGHT

Diversity

We will rush ever on without fear;
Let the goal be far, the flight be fleet!
—James Thomson

Hilda Collens liked celebrating anniversaries and in 1949, a year before the Northern's thirtieth birthday, she seems to have determined on a particularly busy period of preparation. In these eventful months the school took several long strides towards an even brighter future.

The expansion was not dramatic, but it was significant. The annual distribution of awards was held on February 3, with White in the chair. The guest invited to make the presentations was Charles Groves, then conductor of the B.B.C. Northern Orchestra. (This was another example of Miss Collens's ability to win friends, for Groves became a member of the council the following year and has been a staunch friend and supporter of the Northern ever since.) The Easter term ended with a concert conducted by Read, in which Parry's *Blest Pair of Sirens* provided a choral and orchestral climax. There were many formal concerts during the year and both senior and junior orchestras fulfilled "outside" engagements at such places as Rochdale, Oldham, and Urmston. The Student Christian Movement, perhaps heartened by a recent lecture by the Bishop of Manchester, the Rt. Rev. W. D. L. Greer, was now undoubtedly "an integral part of the school" and continued to hold daily prayer meetings. The work of raising funds to help the Barnardo boy went on and the drama department students "acquitted themselves well" in their work.

The school magazine which was published that July had the same familiar green covers with the tasteful gold titling.

73

The layout of the pages was the same and so was the enthusiasm which the magazine radiated. The new editor, Dorothy Pilling, had seen to it that traditions were maintained. There was, however, a slight shift in emphasis. The previous year's editorial had praised the expansion of the school and welcomed the extensions in glowing terms. By now it was apparent that the extensions were not big enough. The magazine commented: "Having adapted itself to its new extensions, the school begins to find that even they are at times inadequate. One hears of horn or violin lessons being given in the secretary's office, or an occasional drama class in the staff canteen, when the congestion becomes acute." These were perhaps the hardest lessons in harmony any school of music might be expected to endure, but the Northern avoided internal dissonance and made do. If only they had the money what might they not do!

The magazine continued:

Plans are now in preparation for further alterations which will result in more studios for lessons or classes, the shortage of which presents an ever-increasing problem of accommodation since the intake of new students exceeds the outflow. As one student was recently overheard to say: "Nobody *ever* wants to leave the Northern School of Music!" One reason for this reluctance may be the well-remembered spirit of friendliness and easy camaraderie which still pervade the whole building.

The semi-official reason for this quality of life at the Northern was given:

The youngest and newest students are speedily made to feel that they matter to the school, and that they form an individual and integral part of the whole complex pattern. This feeling that much depends on each personal unit inculcates a sense of happy responsibility into all members of this busy community and, surely, accounts in no small measure for the success of the school as a corporate body.

Perhaps the ladies of the Northern protested a little too much, and later generations may accuse them of romanticising the Northern (in their literary proselytising, that is), of being loyal to a fault, and of lacking objectivity—a common libel used, objectively, in an attempt to discredit doughty opponents. Although the magazine may be presumed to have been toeing the official line as a good official publication should, the truth was yet with it. Miss Collens had gathered about her a large staff and they had become friends. Some had reconciled themselves to a reduction in salary in order to join Miss Collens at the Northern : all could have received much greater financial rewards elsewhere. A pension fund, as we have seen, had only recently been set up and there could be no thoughts of retirement into affluence. To deny that there were occasional moments of friction or that even the best of friends may sometimes disagree would be to indulge in cosy fantasy. Miss Collens was an individualist surrounded by individualists, but they worked well as a team, united by a love of music and an unshakeable belief in the work of the school. They got on well together and there were no serious differences of opinions to stunt the growth of the Northern.

The students were impressed by the welcoming tone of the school. Some have recorded how, after interviews at other establishments, they had gone on to the Northern expecting another cool encounter with academic authority, only to find that they were received cordially and put at their ease, remarking the prevailing happiness within sight and sound of very hard work. Few of the students ever came to consider that those first impressions were misleading, and though they occasionally grumbled about the benevolent dictatorship of "the workhouse" there was no desire to rebel. Their yoke was easy even if their burdens were heavy and exacting. No dictatorship, however benevolent, could have ensured the spontaneity of the many social events, the vigour of the Present Students' Association, the Student Christian Movement, and the Barnardo boy fund, or the remarkable strength

—not only in numbers—of the Old Students' Association.

Sceptics might question the eulogies heaped upon the Northern but the facts concerned merely with the academic work confound them. The twelve months ending in April 1949 had seen Olga Wilson taking her Mus.B. final at Cambridge, John Pye passing Part I of his Mus.B. final at London, and Gordon Black and Michael Callaghan successfully engaged on external degree courses for London and Dublin respectively. Northern students collected thirty-three L.R.A.M.s: Mary Whitmore (piano) and Pauline Tinsley (singing) were the only performers; the rest of the L.R.A.M.s were for teaching, including five for speech and drama.

There were two licentiates of the Guildhall School: F. O. Platts (speech and drama) and Carol Walker, who gained the Cheshire county music scholarship. There were also many Associated Board certificates. The following year Northern students gained forty-three L.R.A.M.s and again the emphasis was on teaching. The three successful performers were Eugene Collins (piano) and James Calladine and Sylvia Morris (singing). Twenty-three of the L.R.A.M.s were for teaching piano and two, taken by Maureen Hey and J. O'Neill, for speech and drama. Two other drama department students, Joan Clyde-Dean and Ursula Woolfenden, became Guildhall licentiates, Eugene Collins gained an A.R.C.M. to accompany his L.R.A.M., Brenda Arrowsmith won the Cheshire county music scholarship, and the pianist Joyce Favill was awarded the Associated Board gold medal for gaining the highest marks in Britain.

During these two years the academic successes were complemented by a wide range of appointments. Old students took up teaching posts throughout Britain, including schools in Bognor Regis, Portsmouth, Preston, Stockport, Scarborough, Seascale, Leyland, Falmouth, Rhyl, Blackburn, Pendleton, and Manchester. Drama students were also spreading their wings: Arthur Bentley became stage manager of the Cambridge Theatre, London; Brian Hoyle and Enid Openshaw joined repertory companies; and Brian Rawlinson, during study at the Royal Academy of Dramatic Art, had been named R.A.D.A. scholar of his year. The pianist Hubert Harry, one of the most brilliant pianists produced by the school, was reported to be pursuing successfully his studies in Europe.

The school in 1949 was beginning to be much more outward-looking and much more confident than at any time since its incorporation in the precarious days of 1943. The premises had been enlarged and there were now nearly 500 full-time and part-time students. Examination successes were impressive and the Northern's influence had reached beyond the greater Manchester area. In July the holiday course included master classes by the pianist Louis Kentner and lectures by Ellis Keeler. A party from the school travelled to Queenswood School, in Hertfordshire, for the first orchestral training course there under Read's direction. They took part in "a strenuous week" of rehearsals, private lessons, and group coaching in which three orchestras studied scores under Read, Myers Foggin, Richard Austin, George Stratton, Leslie Regan—in between visits to Hatfield House, St Albans, and the London Proms. Horizons were widening: even the annual school picnic ventured as far as Chester, where a sunny day was spent boating, in exploring the old city, or in team games which seem by most accounts to have increased the students' predilection for ice cream.

October saw the arrival of Bernard Shore, Ministry of Education staff inspector of music, and four colleagues to inspect the work of the school. All aspects of the Northern's work were scrutinised and then, after a thorough inspection lasting two weeks, Shore and his assistants went off to prepare their report to the Ministry. While awaiting the outcome, Miss Collens allowed herself hope. She told old students that if the inspectors "reported only one-half of the good things which they said, it must surely augur well for our future".

October was also marked by a remarkable reunion which took the form of a concert of piano music by old students at the Houldsworth Hall. Old friendships were renewed in the packed hall and a clear profit of £55 went to the O.S.A. bursary fund. Marjorie Proudlove opened the programme with Bach's fantasia and fugue in D, then came two movements from Mozart's A major concerto played by Marjorie Hopwood, with Rayson Whalley playing the "orchestral" piano. The novelty of the evening was Poulenc's sonata for eight hands, in which the two pianos were played by Eileen Chadwick, Constance Kay, Irene Wilde, and Gordon Black. Items by Brahms and Granados followed and then, "with Ida Carroll at the first piano and Rayson Whalley at the second, the evening rolled to an exciting finish with the first movement of Beethoven's concerto in C minor".

It was an enjoyable evening, but a concert given at the Albert Hall on November 17 was of much greater moment for the Northern. The milestone passed that night was the school's first performance of *Messiah*. It was the first time the school had ever presented a big choral and orchestral work. It was an "all-Northern" presentation, in that all the performers had strong connections with the school. The four soloists, all students, were Joan Moss (soprano), Hazel Pullen (contralto), Vincent Coates (tenor), and James Calladine. They were coached by Keeler and Irene Wilde. The choir was trained by Gertrude Riall and the orchestra (led by Reginald Stead and with Norman Mansell the principal viola) by Ida Carroll. The historic performance was conducted by "the indefatigable Mr Ernest Read, who, as always, drew from his forces the best that was in them".

After this successful *Messiah* immediate plans were made for an assault on *The Creation* the following May. This, too, was conducted by the indefatigable Read and "the charming naïveté of the music was savoured to the full".

The Ministry took some time in recognising the Northern, but Shore had clearly been impressed, for it was he who presented the prizes at the annual distribution held on January 27, 1950. It was the last such occasion chaired by Mrs Moon,

because she died in December. Miss Collens recorded: "With
the passing of this gracious lady, the school lost one of its
most staunch supporters and I one of my best friends . . . I
think we all loved Mrs Moon and she loved us. She could
ill be spared from this life but the future one must surely be
enriched by her presence."

There were several changes in the membership of the school
council during the period. The Rev. Arthur White, who had
chaired the annual distribution of awards in 1949, and
Alderman Will Melland, one of the Northern's first vice-
presidents, had died just before Mrs Moon. New members
elected to the council in 1950 were Alderman Abraham Moss,
of Manchester City Council, Charles Groves, Mrs Ruth Moon,
the Rev. G. Pusey, rector of Holy Innocents, Fallowfield, and
Mrs Agnes Barker. The new chairman was Clement Gerrard,
head of a building firm, who had been elected to the council
in 1949.

Staff appointments included the return of Leonard Hirsch
to teach violin and to take classes in ensemble playing. John
Hunt was visiting the school each month to give advanced
piano lessons. And Sumner Austin took charge of a new
venture, the opera class. The success of *Messiah* and *The
Creation* came at a time when the drama department was
earning many golden opinions and a fair share of L.R.A.M.s
for its work, and when the orchestras were flourishing. The
Northern could dream of "the close co-operation of dramatic,
vocal and orchestral forces in a full-length performance of
(perhaps) *A Midsummer Night's Dream* (with Mendelssohn's
lovely incidental music); of *Dido and Aeneas* or *The Marriage
of Figaro*."

This consummation was not long in the wishing. By 1951,
with many successful concerts (including another *Messiah*)
and plays behind them, the staff and students of the Northern
could prepare themselves to stage an opera for the first time.
The Bartered Bride was chosen and, after many months of
preparation, the veil was lifted on July 3, 1952, at the Lesser

Free Trade Hall. Austin, with the assistance of Irene Wilde, produced the opera and Aylmer Buesst conducted, but it was undoubtedly a team effort. Ida Carroll had trained the orchestra, Adelaide Trainor was the stage manager and make-up artist, and the ballet dancers (there being no lack of ambition) were trained by Helena Walley. The bold, colourful venture into opera was well received on the first night and at the two performances which followed. Miss Collens's only regret "was that we had not booked the hall for more nights, as we could have sold out many times".

Miss Collens had missed the final stages of rehearsal for *The Bartered Bride*. Illness had meant her enforced absence from the school for several weeks, but she "felt very proud of the way in which our school has been carried on in my absence. Nothing seems to have suffered. Staff and students have combined to see that everything has worked as usual, and for this I am very grateful."

"Illness", she wrote, "is never pleasant, but it does give one time to think and count one's blessings. I am sure that one of my greatest blessings is the love which you all shower upon me; your goodness has been overwhelming and I thank each one for the thoughts and prayers which have helped me so much."

Recovery was slow, but she was greatly heartened by news she received on June 5 as she lay in bed. It was that the Burnham Committee had agreed at last to give graduate status to Northern students who fulfilled the "special conditions established by the school". No longer would old students and local authorities be in doubt about the validity of training at the Northern School of Music. No more need Miss Collens write about references to Ministry circulars. Those who passed successfully through the graduate course would in future be able to don hoods of green and gold and add the letters G.N.S.M. after their names.[1]

This welcome news, the outcome of Shore's original inspec-

---

[1] The first to do so were Edwina Ambrose, Margaret Gifford, John Greenwood, Jack Grimshaw, Dorothy Hayward, Winifred Lee, Sheila Middlebrooke, Jean Watson, and Keith Webb.

tion and subsequent visits to the school when he offered help and suggestions, encouraged Miss Collens. Her strength seemed to grow daily and by June 21 she was able to attend the annual junior concert at the Houldsworth Hall. The production of *The Bartered Bride* provided further encouragement towards recovery.

Concerts, recitals, plays, oratorios, and now an opera and graduate status were adequate testimony to the outside world that all was well with the Northern. So, academically and musically, it was. But the financial reckonings would have told a different story. Miss Collens and the council, under the leadership of Gerrard, were shrewd housekeepers, well used to making the "workhouse's" meagre income go a long way. Despite all their efforts the Northern was still in a perilous financial condition which added to Miss Collens's anxieties. She must also have had doubts about her health. Ever since the bad attack of shingles in 1940 Miss Collens had been having regular injections against various side-effects. Years of hard work and worry had exacted their toll and Miss Collens's health was no longer robust. She relied on her deputy, Miss Carroll, for much of the administrative work and relied increasingly on her counsel.

Miss Collens's enthusiasm, however, was undiminished. She urged on attempts to gain status as qualified teachers for members of the speech and drama course. She and the council approached the various authorities for financial aid. She replied firmly to criticisms made by some old students that some of the school's intimacy had been lost: "Obviously this is true, but [the school's] fundamental principles of hard work and good comradeship are lasting, and the experience and thrill of sharing in the performance of major works could not have existed in the days when we numbered only nine, happy as those days were!" Miss Collens fought hard for her school. "I always feel that [it] is founded upon a 'Rock' which is higher than ourselves, and this Rock will never fail us so long as we also do our part."

The Rock on which the school was founded was firm

F

enough, but the greatly enlarged superstructure was highly susceptible to the remorseless buffetings of icy economic winds. Faith was not enough without financial aid, as Miss Collens well knew. Old students had been generous, never failing to respond to requests for help, but the amounts they could give presented no permanent solution to the school's financial ills. The Northern had "gone public" in 1943 to banish any suggestion of commercialism and to create a situation in which some form of public aid might be possible. While the Northern, after nine persuasive years, had been granted graduate status, the financial aid from local authorities was meagre.

In 1951 the school made a loss of £51, in 1952 the deficit was £104, and in 1953 it had further increased to £173. The trend was disturbing.

While the Royal Manchester College of Music, possessed of a royal charter and the prestige that goes with it, might attract the cream of performers and the financial attentions of the Treasury and other discerning bodies, the Northern had to see to its own monetary salvation. It had a reputation for producing fine teachers of music. There had also been several outstanding performers. The work of the speech and drama department had attracted much praise and many examination successes. But Miss Collens eschewed any chasing of glamour or that elusive quality known today as "prestige". She considered that the school had a big job to do and she saw that the school got on with it.

Such an approach does not win over hard-pressed finance committees of local authorities. And yet there was hope. Miss Collens had written to the Ministry of Education about grants. In March 1953 the Ministry had replied that it could not help. So informal approaches were made to Norman Fisher, chief education officer of Manchester, seeking advice on financial matters. At a meeting in September, Fisher was sympathetic and promised to investigate the Northern's financial position. Miss Collens and Miss Carroll also had talks with Will Griffiths, M.P. for the Manchester Exchange division, who undertook to consult other local M.P.s about any plans to help the school.

Far back, through the creeks and inlets it had been making during the past few months, came some indication of the silent main. At its meeting on April 1, 1954, the school council, headed by Gerrard, welcomed the news that Manchester was increasing its grant to £500 a year.

It was only a trickle, but it was a sign that the tide had turned and as such it was gladly received, not only for its cash value but for the recognition which the grant implied.

Three months later, in July 1954, a serious road accident brought about a change in the Northern's domestic affairs. Because of the indisposition of its driver, a Manchester corporation bus ran out of control, knocking down a cyclist and killing a woman who had run to the doorway of No. 95A Oxford Road in the hope of avoiding the vehicle. She was pinned to the wall. The Dolcis shoe shop at 95A was damaged and the proprietors decided to close the shop altogether. Miss Carroll went to London to see Upsons, the owners of the premises, who all along had been kindly landlords to the Northern. With magnanimity worthy of the Cheeryble brothers, Upsons agreed to let the whole building to the school at a nominal rent. The school would be allowed to sub-let the shop at 95A at any rent it could get—without the Northern's having to pay any more to Upsons. The shop was let soon after to the Beanstalk Shelving Company, who were to continue as the school's tenants until 1969.

Most of the students and old students were unaware of these extra-musical problems which had been exercising the minds and energies of Miss Collens and her deputy. During this period of financial strain the work had continued to expand. For the school's second operatic essay, Strauss's *Die Fledermaus* was chosen and four performances were given at the Lesser Free Trade Hall as the climax to the summer term of 1953.

As with *The Bartered Bride*, the production was by Austin,

the orchestra was trained by Ida Carroll, and the chorus by
Irene Wilde. Adelaide Trainor was the stage manager and
Buesst the conductor. "There was", we are told, "some admir-
able singing and convincing acting in this most delightful
opera, which pursued its merry way with almost the authentic
Viennese sparkle."

This was followed in July 1954 by three performances of
The Marriage of Figaro.

> The orchestra faced the onerous task of playing some of
> the loveliest and most difficult music in existence; the
> rarest qualities of musicianship are needed to reveal the
> superb poise and consummate artistry of a Mozart operatic
> score. Under the sensitive direction of Mr Buesst they made
> a brave showing, while the attainments of the cast in sing-
> ing and in characterisation spoke volumes for the careful
> and devoted coaching they had received.

The school found enough encouragement in the experience
to press on with *The Magic Flute* for its 1955 production.

Opera was the most demanding of the Northern's many
projects, but it was only one aspect of the work. Other notable
events included broadcasts by the Northern School of Music
Wind Ensemble, and on June 3, 1954, the first major school
concert (at the Houldsworth Hall) was devoted entirely to
chamber music, an indication of the number of students
learning orchestral instruments. The programme included
movements from the Mendelssohn octet, Brahms's string sextet,
Op. 36, *On Wenlock Edge*, Vaughan Williams's song cycle
for tenor, string quartet and piano, and a Haydn divertimento
for wind quintet. The "main" work was Bach's D minor
concerto for piano and strings.

Another sign of the growing diversity of what had once
been a piano school was the first orchestral concert by members
of the junior school, whose rehearsals were confined to one
hour a week. Ida Carroll conducted the concert on March 18,

1955, which included Mendelssohn's G minor piano concerto played by Victoria Sumner "with a real sense of style", and the first movement of Haydn's trumpet concerto played by Ian Brown.

On March 19, 1954, Charles Groves conducted the school's performance of *Messiah* at the Houldsworth Hall. The soloists were Pamela Rhodes, Patricia Wallace, John O'Sullivan, and Albert Haskayne. George Fisher, describing the performance, wrote that "Mr William Hardwick played the organ part magnificently despite the somewhat collapsible nature of this particular neglected example of a noble instrument". However, Groves seems to have brought the best out of the singers and instrumentalists.

Mounting enthusiasm was the keynote of the evening— on the part of the audience, the performers and the con- ductor, who drew from his forces all they could give and performed his task with such a cumulative sense of climax that it seemed only poetic justice that his baton should fly out of his hand and break into two pieces on the final chord of the "Amen" chorus.

Northern musicians were enhancing the school's reputation in many parts of Britain. The flow of teachers was unabated. The flow of performers was increasing.

Organists had been appointed to various churches including St Philip's, Hulme, Hazel Grove Congregational, Gatley Congregational, St John's, Pendlebury, Stockton Heath Parish, and St Margaret's, Dunham Massey. The Coronation year of 1953 had seen several old students engaged at summer holiday resorts: the violinist Joan Farrow was at St Anne's, and the bassoonist Leonard Latchford at Buxton, while Ceridwen Jones was Gorsedd harpist at the Royal National Eisteddfod at Rhyl. Another harpist, Beryl Eves, played with the Scottish National Orchestra of which another old student, Erik Knussen, a double-bass player, had been appointed orchestral manager. The pianist William Rayner was on active musical service aboard the *Queen Mary*, Vincent Billington was appointed concert pianist to the Royal Engineers Orchestra (in those days of compulsory National Service), and Peter Waddington was spending his spare time as the *Evesham Standard*'s music critic after lecturing at Birmingham University extra-mural department. John Crosdale (trumpet) had joined the Scottish National Orchestra, and Margaret Moore (oboe) became the Liverpool Philharmonic's cor anglais.

Within the next eighteen months the number of instrumentalists in British orchestras, either permanently or as freelances, had risen dramatically. After six months with the Yorkshire Symphony Orchestra, Harry Brennand became the B.B.C. Midland's first horn. Joan Farrow was with the Bournemouth Municipal Orchestra, and Jean Soni (viola) with the B.B.C. Northern. Freelance work with professional orchestras was undertaken by many Northern-trained string players, including David Bell (double bass), Anne Holt, Geoffrey York (Leslie Jones String Orchestra), and Anne Brindley, Audrey Waterhouse and Sheila Frankland (Manchester String Orchestra).

Apart from Vincent Billington, the army had claimed many old students for its orchestras. These included Gerald Brinnen (double bass), Kenneth Monks (horn), John Morgan (violin), Martin Somers (oboe), Ivor Griffiths (clarinet), and John Alker (bassoon).

Several singers were advancing their careers. Pauline McCormick had joined the D'Oyly Carte Opera Company, Hazel Pullen and Albert Haskayne had been soloists with the Liverpool Philharmonic Orchestra, and other singers heard at public concerts and musical events included Donald Rutter, Edith Chatterton, James Calladine, Pauline Tinsley, and Vincent Coates. Of the Northern's many pianists, Hubert Harry, who had made a distinguished début at the Royal Festival Hall, London in 1952, was building up an enviable reputation as a recitalist. He was now on the staff of the

Geneva Conservatoire, but in October 1954 he returned to London for two engagements at the Festival Hall. At the first he was the soloist in Tchaikovsky's B flat minor concerto in a concert given by the London Philharmonic under Stanley Pope.

For the second, a recital of Bach, Beethoven, Brahms, Chopin and Bartok, Miss Collens led a strong contingent from the school and received "convincing aural evidence of [Harry's] steadily maturing talent and musicianship". The recital was followed by a grand reunion in the foyer of the Festival Hall and then by "a lively supper party" before Miss Collens and the Manchester delegation headed for Euston for the overnight train back to Manchester. Work at Oxford Road began, as usual, early the same morning.

Former members of the speech and drama course were winning deserved attention. Anne Powell had become a peripatetic teacher with Manchester Speech Clinic; Eileen Derbyshire was playing leading parts with the Century Theatre; Mary Griffiths had played in a London production of Dorothy Sayers' *The Man Born to be King*; Enid Openshaw was teaching at Skellfield School, Yorkshire; and Arthur Bentley was "fully occupied" with work in all aspects of drama, including the straight theatre, pantomime, radio, television, and films. And by 1955 the Ministry of Education added the Northern School to the list of institutions recognised for the training of teachers in speech and drama. Until now the only recognised courses had been in London.

Such, by 1955, was the remarkable growth of the school and the network of students throughout Britain that, as the magazine proudly claimed, "its effect on musical life in general is undeniable". The magazine continued:

There is hardly a county which does not possess schools where our members are doing sound, resourceful work carrying much responsibility; most of the representative orchestras of the country number some of our past students whose first introduction to this very rewarding branch of music-making took place in the Friday afternoon orchestral rehearsals; our singers and instrumentalists find many and various fields for the exercise of their talents; past members of the Speech and Drama course are doing excellent work, both in the teaching profession and on the stage. It is heartening and inspiring to observe these healthy offshoots from the parent stem, and to realise that the personal effort of every individual fits inevitably and felicitously into the whole symmetrical design.

CHAPTER NINE

Life's end

As falls the silent dew,
With evening's fading light,
So may the gentle gift of sleep
Descend on us tonight.

—Vesper by Walter Carroll

By 1955 the school was giving more public concerts than ever before, its musical reputation was rising steadily and so were the numbers of examinations successes, student activities, and appointments gained. No less a personage than the Earl of Derby presented the awards at the annual distribution on January 25 at the Houldsworth Hall. Following the satisfaction of all concerned in the school production of *Figaro*, preparations for four stage performances of *The Magic Flute* were well under way.

But in 1955 the Northern was happy but poor, so poor in fact that the prospect of bankruptcy seemed more than just a possibility. After a loss of £279 in 1954, the school was facing a deficit of £947 for 1955. Miss Collens, frail and ailing, was still active and hopeful, but financial worries were undoubtedly putting a severe strain on her. As Michael Kennedy has stated,[1] it was a period when the costs of running the Royal Manchester College of Music were increasing sharply. Yet the Treasury grant to the R.M.C.M. for 1953–54 was £7,500. The Northern received no Treasury grant at all, and its costs, too, were rising steeply. In 1954, as we have seen, Manchester Corporation agreed to increase its grant to the Northern to £500 (at a time, incidentally, when it proposed—apparently

[1] *The History of the Royal Manchester College of Music, 1893–1972.*

in a moment of municipal mischief—to reduce its aid of £225 to the R.M.C.M!). In January 1955 the Northern heard that Cheshire had decided to make a grant of £25 a year.

Even the Northern School's pension fund had been "borrowed". At around 11 o'clock one morning, a stranger came into the school and was greeted by Miss Carroll. The stranger said he was inspecting the premises because he was from a firm of auctioneers who were selling No. 93 Oxford Road that very afternoon. It was news to Miss Carroll, who quickly passed word to Miss Collens, whose surprise was just as great. Surprise was soon replaced by action. The Northern was in debt and in no position to start bidding for property, but there was something in the pension fund kitty. An outrageous idea crossed the minds of Miss Collens and Miss Carroll. Many phone calls were made that morning to members of the council and to friends of the Northern. At 3 p.m. Miss Collens and Miss Carroll were at an auction room in Fountain Street when the properties in the Oxford Road block were put up for sale. The first was knocked down to the nominee of a London group. So were the second and third. The fourth lot, No. 93 Oxford Road—part of the Northern's little empire—also brought a bid from the London nominee. A counter-bid was made immediately by Roger Carter, honorary treasurer of the school. It was a close-run thing, but the Northern had managed to buy No. 93, and the pension fund had been "invested".

Miss Collens was relieved that another crisis had been averted and that once again her faith had been rewarded. Such financial brinkmanship, however, was not a matter from which Miss Collens could draw any comfort. Something would have to be done.

During the year Miss Collens and Miss Carroll had discussions, following representations made by Will Griffiths, with the Parliamentary Secretary to the Minister of Education. It was established, at last, that the Northern School of Music was a college of national and not merely local status. The result of this, and the help given by J. H. Rathbone, of Manchester Corporation, was that the Northern felt that it had justified its existence. Advance balance sheets were supplied to Manchester education committee, as requested.

Approaches by the Royal Manchester College of Music were made during this period and the question of amalgamation was discussed. The rivalry between the two establishments had been manifest for some time. The college, Hallé's "royal" baby, had grown strong and influential, but the Northern School council felt "that the two institutions differed too widely in character, personality, and method for a satisfactory connection to be possible".

The self-interest evident in this decision was enlightened. Whatever its educational achievements, the Northern was in a parlously weak financial position. Miss Collens's fears that in any "amalgamation" the Northern's widely differing traditions would be submerged were understandable. It seemed unlikely that the college would relish any idea of change any more than the Northern School would sacrifice the independence it had fought so hard to maintain. The Northern was not prepared to cede any sovereignty to the college. Whatever might happen, Miss Collens was determined that the Northern would have some say in any decisions which affected its future. As a subsidiary of the Royal Manchester College of Music it was unlikely to have any.

Talks with Manchester Corporation went ahead. The Northern needed help quickly, but it was clear that any large increase in Manchester's financial support would only follow long negotiations. Inevitably there would be conditions and agreement on these was unlikely to come swiftly.

On October 9 Walter Carroll died at the age of 86. He had been bedfast for some time, but his mind had retained its agility. Only four years earlier he had written a small book on how he came to write, for his two daughters, the very successful piano pieces, *Scenes at a Farm*. His friendship was still a great source of inspiration to Miss Collens, who was saddened by loss of one of her greatest friends. The school magazine recorded:

Large numbers of our old students will have vivid
memories of that lovable genial figure who for so long gave
unstintingly of his many talents in the cause of music. He
combined with his purely musical abilities a keen analytical
mind and an irrepressible sense of humour which is surely
part of the key to his never-failing appeal to youth. It is
significant that his greatest work lay in his development of
music in the Manchester schools, and still more in that
flood of compositions which revolutionised pianoforte
teaching and which, in their profound understanding of
the child mind, are works of genius. Perhaps the world-wide
popularity of these lovely miniatures, and their never-failing
appeal to the children whom he so loved, form his most
fitting memorial; in them is permanently enshrined the
essence of that rare personality.

Mary Lockley (formerly Dunkerley) wrote:

I remember very clearly indeed the day that his name
became known to me. I was about seven years old and had
been given a most exciting book of music—pictures on the
cover, interesting titles inside and the pieces . . . ! *Purple
Heather* opened magic casements for me then and still does
after having heard it played countless times. Although Dr
Carroll did wonderful pioneer work in so many directions
in organising teachers' training courses, children's concerts
and music in schools, to mention a few, his greatest work in
my opinion was his music for pianoforte beginners. He has
had numerous imitators but no-one before him had written
real music for the absolute beginner.

Dr Carroll was an approachable man, glad always to
help students starting a professional career by putting suitable work in their way whenever possible, and by welcoming visitors with problems at his room at the Education
Offices.

A memory shared, I feel sure, by many is of the sound of laughter coming from the hall in which he was lecturing at the early Holiday Courses. No dull lectures from him!

Two months later, on December 9, John W. Johnson died. The school had lost another loyal friend. Despite the loyalty of her staff, Miss Collens must have felt the loneliness as, one by one, her friends died. There was consolation, for her, in knowing that they had passed to the higher life, but age and ill-health had wearied her. Although she remained enthusiastic and proud, she relied more and more on the energies of her deputy, Ida Carroll. Christmas passed off brightly, though, with the usual student jollity and the traditional round of concerts and parties. Miss Collens herself was feeling happier, for news of a generous gift of money from an old student had reached her at the very time she was discussing the school's overdraft with the bank manager. The only condition was that the name of the donor should not be disclosed. This anonymous gift had been quite unexpected, and it averted a serious financial crisis, if only temporarily. The talks with Manchester could go on free from acute financial pressure.

The first major event of 1956 was the performance of *Elijah* at the Houldsworth Hall on February 27. George Fisher reported:

> The soloists were Grace Yerkess, Patricia Wallace, John Hughes, and Albert Haskayne, who sang as though they were experienced in drama—as though the School's operatic productions had prepared them. . . . There were no two ways about it; Albert Haskayne *was* Elijah—a very good Elijah too—and the choir became in turn the Israelites, the priests of Baal, and the thankful children of God with great effect. The orchestral support was unfailing, and the artistry of the solo instrumentalists of a high order.

Fisher's report was written for "home" consumption, and if there was anything at fault he failed to mention it. One is left, however, with the impression that it was "a grand concert". "The orchestra, choir, and soloists did surpassing credit to their trainers. Mr Charles Groves, our conductor, on this occasion, brought the best out of us all." Work on Nicolai's opera *The Merry Wives of Windsor*, chosen for the school's annual production that summer, could proceed with confidence.

In February the school council was told that £2,000 which had been given to the Northern was to provide a scholarship in memory of Walter Carroll. A condition of the trust was that in the event of the association's being dissolved, the money could be returned under a deed of gift. The council decided at this meeting to use the money to establish a trust fund in the name of Walter Carroll.

The discussions with Manchester Corporation, begun in earnest the previous November, seemed to be going well. Miss Collens was confident that the Northern might be accepted as a Manchester institution. But her ill-health, aggravated by a heart condition, had become increasingly obvious. She was often obliged to take to her bed and leave the administration to Ida Carroll. There were fears that she would be unequal to the strain of the long negotiations that lay ahead.

In April she seemed to be gaining strength, though her staff were watchful. April 27 was as busy as all Fridays at the Northern. Miss Collens saw many of the students and coped with the day's routine. She went home tired but happy, although she did mention that she did not feel well.

Monday was the start of another term. The school assembled as usual. Miss Carroll broke the news to the students: Miss Collens, whom some had seen last Friday, was dead. She had died of a heart attack on Saturday, April 28. A few short prayers were said and the assembly was dismissed. Many of the staff and students were weeping: it had been a great shock. Some members of staff learned of Miss Collens's death only minutes before the assembly; as they arrived at the school Miss Carroll had told them. The end, so long expected, had in reality been unexpected.

Miss Carroll and her colleagues decided that, whatever was to become of the school, it must carry on as normally as possible. Classes were held that Monday, but sadness pervaded the school. One staff member recalled that "it was the worst week the school has ever known. Everyone was so upset. It was such a great blow, and the Northern School of Music without Miss Collens was unthinkable."

On Wednesday, May 2, the gentle spring sunshine filled the nave of Holy Innocents' Church, Fallowfield, and cast its soft warmth on the green and golden floral tributes. Staff, students, and her many friends gathered in the church for the quiet farewell. Hilda Collens, who lived and died in the faith and fear of God, had herself passed to the higher life. "Our sadness", Mary Lockley wrote, "must be for ourselves only, for all that we shall miss; we shall ever give thanks for all that we have gained from the life and love of such a great woman."

Many tributes were paid then to Hilda Collens. Macpherson's widow, Mrs L. F. Macpherson, said: "She was a wonderful person in many ways and, as we all know, the school was her life and its welfare meant everything to her." Dr. M. G. Clarke, wrote: "Her college bears her enduring witness as does the whole musical culture of the North of England, for without the teachers she trained—when no-one else was doing so—where would that culture be? She blazed the trail which the royal institutions and universities are only now beginning to follow."

In an appreciation of Miss Collens, among several written by distinguished musicians soon after her death, is this by Clifford Curzon:

Miss Hilda Collens was, to all who came in contact with her, an example of rare devotion to an ideal. Having conceived, early in her life, the idea of founding a school of music, she dedicated herself with unusual self-sacrifice to its establishment, never tiring under the exacting demands of a principalship in the real sense of the word. But remarkable as were her gifts as an executive, she was no less valued as a friend; her self-imposed and strong sense of duty never obscured that understanding of human weaknesses and idiosyncrasies which should be innate in every fine teacher. And now, in passing, she has achieved through all those who came in personal and musical contact with her, the special immortality of the true pedagogue.

Hilda Collens was always admirably forward-looking and open to new ideas, and she never hesitated to invite artists from the concert platform to criticise the work of the school, even though such criticism might on occasion be in conflict with her own teaching. When she first asked me, more than twenty years ago, to what was then called the Manchester branch of the Matthay School of Music, to lecture for the M.T.A. (Music Teachers' Association), to give a class for some of her pupils, and to give herself an occasional private lesson, I was deeply impressed by the open-mindedness of all connected with the school. I found the standards expected of and achieved by the teachers and pupils often superior to those found in older and more prominent institutions. Later years brought new problems : extensions to the premises, the fight for graduate status, and most important (and irksome!) the need of greater financial aid if the school was to continue its important work on the level dictated by the ideals of its Principal. These difficulties were faced by Miss Collens in a spirit of extraordinary faith, and many of them were overcome by her determined resolution. Being a deeply religious woman, she did not expect and would not have wished for an easy path; we can only honour her, in remembrance, for her fortitude in fighting the odds inevitably bound up with the establishing of any educational institution.

Many little personal things come to mind . . . I remember, for instance, the key to the school that Hilda always gave me on my visits to Manchester so that I could practise after school hours, and roam freely from piano to piano; and the character behind the remark that, much as she would like to

The Hilda Collens memorial window
by courtesy of the Manchester Evening News

The Foundation Stone of the new College

come to my concert, she could never hear me on Sunday afternoons as she had a standing engagement—an engagement which I later discovered to be the self-imposed taking of a Bible class for small children.

The thought of a visit to Oxford Road without Hilda Collens is indeed sad; but she would have rejoiced to feel that her life's work might be continued there where she gave far more than she ever received—as, in any case, it *will* be continued by those who studied with and knew her.

Hilda Collens did not seek the great prizes; but in thinking of her we are reminded of Portia's phrase: "How far that little candle throws his beams." Her life was a triumph of integrity and singleness of purpose.

CHAPTER TEN

Attacca

*A clash of doctrines is not a
disaster—it is an opportunity.*

—Alfred North Whitehead

Ida Carroll and Irene Wilde were with Miss Collens at her home in Sale when she died. There was a lot to do that sad Saturday morning. Timetables had to be rearranged, staff had to be notified, and there were the sorrowful tasks at the school of checking any outstanding paperwork and arranging the funeral.

Shock had not yet given way to mourning, and the women worked well into Saturday night and returned to the tasks on Sunday. The most important thing was to see that, as far as possible, there was no serious interruption in the life of the Northern. The devotion they accorded Miss Collens demanded no less. Miss Carroll, who had been Miss Collens's deputy for several years, took full charge. One member of the staff said: "There was no-one else on the staff who could have done it, and she just got on with what had to be done."

At its meeting in May, the council confirmed Miss Carroll as acting Principal from April 28, the date of Miss Collens's death. Members of the council, under the leadership of Gerrard, did not wish for there to be any break. Talks with Manchester about the Northern's future were in intermittent progress. Radical changes of policy, even if they had been thought desirable, would have been unlikely to hasten the closer contacts with Manchester which the school council wanted.

Outwardly there were few signs of change. The production of *The Merry Wives of Windsor* went well. So did the holiday course. It was opened by Rayson Whalley, who lectured on the function of the piano in modern orchestras; Marjorie Proudlove discussed piano teaching; Kathleen Forster gave classes in string playing; Dr Annie Warburton lectured about school music; and the master classes in piano were given by John Hunt. A concert in memory of Miss Collens, given on July 12 and conducted by Ernest Read, included a performance of Fauré's *Requiem* in which the soloists were Pamela Rhodes and Albert Haskayne, who a few months later joined the staff as a full-time teacher of solo singing. More than twenty teachers trained at the Northern gained appointments to schools in various parts of the country; instrumental players, too, were having success—including the flautist Douglas Townshend, with the Hallé, Liverpool Philharmonic, and B.B.C. Northern orchestras; Sylvia Schneck, as the second oboe at Liverpool; and the clarinettist Frank Holdsworth, who was playing regularly with the Hallé. Members of the speech and drama department added to the school's reputation, appearing on television and in repertory. Joy Jung, the wife of Rayson Whalley, was one of the many members of the department who went on to teach. She was chosen to direct a pioneer scheme at Princess Road evening centre, Manchester. The classes, which helped students to improve their speech and brush up on etiquette, were so successful that they were featured on B.B.C. television.

On January 29, 1957, Sir Steuart Wilson presented the awards at the annual distribution and Miss Carroll was able to give an encouraging report on the progress of the school. She had reason for optimism, for by now the talks with representatives of Manchester education committee had produced a two-stage plan. It had been argued that Scheme 1, which was for closer co-operation between the school and the education committee, would be implemented immediately. The second stage, known as Scheme 2, would begin in September 1958 or as soon as possible after then. The second stage would mean much wider co-operation and, being a more ambitious plan, would necessitate the appointment of a principal within twelve months. The discussions begun in November 1955 had borne fruit. In February 1957 a letter was sent to J. K. Elliot, who was now Manchester's chief education officer, outlining the Northern School council's views on the proposals. The council had agreed unanimously that the name, status, and "high-level work in both performance and teaching" should be maintained, that the appointment of Principal and any additional members of staff should be those in sympathy with the methods and traditions of the Northern School, and that, as far as possible, present members of staff should be retained. The council was also unanimous in agreeing that all parts of the school's curriculum should be retained, that the four scholarships—the Walter Carroll, Stewart Macpherson, Frederick Moore and Ernest Read—should be continued "both in name and kind", and that the Old Students' Association and its offshoots—such as the bursary fund—maintained.

On April 16 a meeting between representatives of the Northern School and the Royal Manchester College of Music was arranged by the new Vice-Chancellor of Manchester University, Professor (later Sir) William Mansfield Cooper, who was also chairman of the R.M.C.M. council (who was unable to attend). The R.M.C.M. representatives wished to know the Northern's views on the possibility of closer co-operation or even amalgamation. The matter was discussed at length, but the Northern School representatives felt that nothing could be done. They preferred to continue their independent negotiations with Manchester education committee. If any useful purpose could be served by another meeting with the college, the Northern School was willing to arrange it. Any initiative now lay with the Northern.

Two months later a suggestion by the college that, in closer co-operation between the schools, the Northern should be responsible for all teacher-training of graduates, was discussed and dismissed. Gerrard and the council could not contemplate amalgamation on those terms. They preferred to press on with Manchester education committee in exploring the implications of the wider and more adventurous proposals agreed some months before. Soon after, Manchester raised its grant to the Northern to £750. It was very welcome, for in 1956 the school had sustained a loss of £922. In 1957 this was reduced to £517.

Apart from the complexities of critical negotiations, the year 1957 saw many other developments. Of these the most important was a change in the syllabus of the graduate course, bringing the Northern into line with other music colleges in making the diploma an internal one. In October Miss Carroll reported to the council that the new syllabus had been approved by Bernard Shore and also by Miss C. C. Bell, responsible for teacher-training at the Ministry of Education, and that it was now awaiting the approval of the Burnham Committee.

The 1957 holiday course included lectures by Clifford Curzon, Michael Kennedy, Noel Long, Dorothy Pilling, Dr Annie Warburton, and Sir Steuart Wilson. Ambroise Thomas's *Mignon* was the unusual choice for the opera production, once again prepared by Sumner Austin and conducted by Buesst. The title role was sung by Norma Day, Philine by June Glynne-Jones, Wilhelm by James Hyde, and Lothario by John Shaw.

Hilda Collens was not forgotten. Part of the money raised for the memorial fund, established soon after her death, had been used to commission a portrait of the founder by Ray Howorth and the picture had been unveiled on January 29 by Ernest Read. Many concerts were given in aid of the fund which in 1957 was merged with the O.S.A. bursary fund. September 24, Miss Collens's birthday, was designated Founder's Day, when old students were invited to visit the school.

A concert in aid of the memorial fund was arranged on November 12 by Hazel Pullen who, despite a throat infection following influenza, also sang songs by Spohr and Brahms. Others taking part were the singer Sheila Fletcher, the pianists Rita Imisson and Mary Whitmore, and the clarinettist Ronald Wright.

Later that month the speech and drama department gave, as part of the Manchester University Arts Festival, performances of *The Snow Queen*, an adaptation by Suria Magito and Rudolph Weil of Hans Andersen's story. Gerda was played by Brenda Elder, who received much praise. Joy Whalley (formerly Jung) noted: "The smoothness of the production (by Adelaide Trainor) was indicative of good team work. . . . The production was undoubtedly a great triumph for the department. Without a permanent theatre their work is hampered, yet when they appear on a stage this drawback is not in the least obvious."

The Christmas concert on December 6 included the choral *Christmas Cantata* by Geoffrey Bush and a sonata for flute and piano by Thomas Pitfield played by Guy Ratcliffe and Vincent Billington.

The annual awards on February 4, 1958, were presented by Mansfield Cooper, with Gerrard in the chair. The invitation had presumably come during the discussions with the college. The chairman of the R.M.C.M. council presenting awards to graduates of the Northern; surely on either side there was appreciation of the irony of the situation—and with it grounds for hope!

There were indeed. In 1958, after three years of debate between the Northern School and Manchester education committee, some headway was being gained. On March 31 Miss Carroll reported to the Northern School council that Manchester had agreed to raise its grant from £750 to £1,000; Cheshire had promised to increase its contribution tenfold, from £25 to £250; Salford had agreed to give more; and Lancashire was reviewing its grant. (Soon after, Lancashire increased its grant from £300 to £500.[1])

At that same meeting the council decided unanimously to

---

[1] The school's loss for 1958 had risen to £1,041.

appoint Miss Carroll Principal. Announcing the decision taken
nearly two years after the death of Miss Collens, Gerrard said :
"I cannot explain why we have been so long in electing her
Principal, but I can assure you that the decision was made
unanimously."

The council, under the chairmanship of Gerrard, then comprised Curzon, Freer, Groves, Read, W. Philip Lockley,
Gordon Thorne, John C. Withers, Abraham Moss, Allan
Wicks, Arthur J. Moon, Mrs Ruth Moon, Mrs Agnes Barker,
the Rev. B. L. Barnby, and Mrs Lockett.

The delay in appointing Miss Carroll Principal, although it
could not have been admitted at the time, seems to have been
caused by deference to Manchester education committee. If
the Northern had no Principal, the committee would have
more scope in making suggestions about the Northern's future.
Principals, once appointed, have certain rights. If Manchester
were to suggest a reorganised school with adequate financial
arrangements, it might also wish to have a voice in the selection of a Principal. This, we must charitably assume, was one
of the reasons for the council's procrastination. In March 1958,
however, it had become obvious that any solution was many
years away. Miss Carroll's appointment began on April 1, the
day after the council meeting.

After a performance of Dyson's *The Canterbury Pilgrims*
at the Houldsworth Hall on May 15, four performances at
the Lesser Free Trade Hall in July of *The Daughter of the
Regiment*, and professorial recitals by John Hunt, Leonard
Hirsch and Ellis Keeler, the school could enjoy its summer
break well satisfied with the way standards had been maintained.

In the autumn the council noted that the school had lost
£1,000 in the year, but there had been an increase in fees and
the number of applications from students wishing to join the
school was encouragingly high. Miss Carroll reported that she
had received many contributions of money from grateful
parents and other friends.

Support for the Northern was growing, but its problems

could not be considered in isolation from the rest of music education in the region. Approaches to local authorities, notably Manchester, had been made by the Northern School. The Royal College, apparently, had financial problems of its own and had made its own approaches to various bodies, including the Treasury. At the instigation of Percy Lord, chief education officer for Lancashire, a meeting was held on December 10 to discuss the future of music education in South-east Lancashire. To these talks were invited representatives of Cheshire, Manchester, Salford, the R.M.C.M., and also of Lancashire and the Northern School of Music. The Northern's representatives, led by Gerrard and Miss Carroll, again made it clear that however great the need for financial aid the Northern was not prepared to consider being taken over but they were willing to discuss any proposals which would include the Northern in a much larger scheme.

As if the Northern School did not have enough worries, there was a new threat, this time to the school's very premises. A new road across the city was proposed and the Northern—or at least No. 91 Oxford Road—was on the building line. Gerrard and Miss Carroll had another fight on their hands, for it would have been difficult to find suitable alternative accommodation. (After much thought and even more discussions, the Northern was able eventually to move into No. 99 and move out of 91, which was demolished in 1964 when clearance was made for the Mancunian Way. Anyone with an inkling of the ways of planners, however, will appreciate that in 1958 plans for the road constituted a very serious threat to the Northern's existence.)

A draft scheme for a new college was prepared and on April 23, 1959, Miss Carroll discussed the points raised in it with representatives of the local authorities concerned. The Northern council discussed the draft scheme, which was for one college of 500 full-time students. It would cost an estimated £263,000 to build and £75,000 a year to run. Some members of the council were unconvinced. They felt that there should be a choice of school in Manchester rather than one larger college. For once, there was a lack of unanimity in the council. When the Press gave details of the draft scheme that autumn outsiders may have gained the impression that the new college had been decided on and all but built. As far as the school council was concerned, this impression was erroneous. There were still many things to be thrashed out.

Turning to purely domestic issues, the council decided to inaugurate an award of honorary Fellowship of the Northern School of Music and that the first three awards should be to Miss Carroll, and to Doris Euerby and Beatrice Rollins— two of the original nine students who later joined the staff.

In July, there were pleasant distractions from the seemingly endless talk about the future. There were the delights of Donizetti's *L'Elisir d'Amore*, conducted at the Lesser Free Trade Hall by Aylmer Buesst, and the traditional holiday course in which the lecturers were Wicks, Shore, Annie Warburton, and Gordon Clinton, with the piano master classes being given by Geoffrey Tankard, a professor at the Royal College of Music.

Like Miss Collens before her, Miss Carroll, aided and willingly abetted by her staff, needed little persuasion to mark any anniversary in style, and it seemed that the fortieth anniversary would be the last occasion for really special celebrations. With the creation of a new college in prospect, there would clearly never be a golden jubilee of the Northern School of Music.

Forty years on. The Northern had genuine cause for pride. Far and asunder though many old students may have gone, older and older though the Northern had become, it was neither shorter in wind nor feeble of foot. There were now 150 full-time students, and 550 part-timers, of whom 220 were juniors. And, said Miss Carroll, "we have never had such a waiting list". There were now fifty-six members of the teaching staff.

The celebrations began, so characteristically of the Northern School, with a thanksgiving service at St Ann's Parish Church on September 24 conducted by Canon Eric Saxon, the rector. The service was followed by a recital by Kendall Taylor, one of the school's nine professors of piano, at the Houldsworth Hall. The programme included the first Manchester performance of a Prelude, Elegy and Toccata by Norman Fulton, as well as Bach and two Beethoven sonatas, Opp. 57 and 110. There were also many other concerts, stage productions of *The Bartered Bride*, and an "at home" at which old students were able to meet and reminisce.

The absence of Gerrard, who had died in February, was a sadder aspect of the celebrations. As the council chairman for nine years he had helped to guide the school through a very critical period. Miss Carroll said of him: "He knew that Miss Collens would have rather closed the door than have allowed the standard to drop. Mr Gerrard was a tower of strength, always encouraging to the members of staff, always helpful with advice upon property matters and, above all, always idealistic in upholding the aims of the school." It was he who had led the defence of the Northern's independence. He had been a doughty champion. At its meeting in March the council elected Arthur J. Moon chairman, and welcomed to membership Dr (later Dame) Kathleen Ollerenshaw, of Manchester City Council, and John Richardson.

The reshuffle had been smooth. Moon, who had for some years been a valued adviser and for the last four a member of the council, ensured that nothing endangered the Northern's unanimity. There had been a change of helmsman, but the Northern was following the same course. The waters were noticeably choppier. It was the unchanged policy of the Northern School that, with certain assurances, it would be willing to co-operate in a scheme for a new college owned by the local authorities. One thing it was not prepared to do was to amalgamate as a voluntary college. The Northern's attitude was that the goodwill established by forty years' hard work was an asset which should be considered of equal importance to the work of the R.M.C.M. The Northern had built up this asset of goodwill with very little financial aid while the college had received substantial grants.

For the Northern the name of the proposed new institution was of supreme importance. The Northern felt that, as it had made the first moves towards a new college as an undertaking by local authorities, the name "Northern" should be part of the new college title. At a meeting of the various representatives held in September, a majority favoured the title "Northern College of Music, Manchester". Had the meeting decided not to include the word "Northern", it is unlikely that the Northern School would have taken any further part in the scheme. It was prepared to close down altogether rather than submerge its identity or ideals.

On February 13, 1961, the general outlines of a draft scheme were put before the Northern School council. This provided for the name "The Northern College of Music, Manchester" and for the formation of a governing body. At its meeting in April the council, under Moon's chairmanship, accepted the draft scheme in principle, "reserving the right to comment upon the terms of the legal agreement when the draft is before us".

Moon earlier had put forward to the full committee of representatives preparing the scheme that a neutral principal should be appointed, and that the two existing institutions should continue as separate entities until the new building was completed. This was the wish of the Northern School council, as was its desire for the new college to have completely different colours and emblems. The council also proposed that the names of diplomas awarded in the past should remain unchanged.

In the five years since the death of Miss Collens the Northern had met many crises. In 1955 the school was facing financial ruin; it had been saved by an unexpected gift. In 1956 Miss Collens had died, but Miss Carroll had taken charge and progress had been maintained. In 1955 the Northern had been worrying about the present. In 1961 it was still worrying. It was for the future it was fighting.

CHAPTER ELEVEN

Progress

*There is no prejudice that the work of art
does not finally overcome.*

—André Gide

The thought of meetings followed by more meetings is daunting, especially as they involved the representatives, those elected and those paid, of four important local authorities; and that they exercised the minds and memoranda of committee clerks, clerks, and officials high, intermediate, and lowly; that they did not leave the Treasury untaxed nor the Ministry of Education uninstructed. As the proposed scope of the proposed college grew even larger, so the proposed membership of the interim governing body (thankfully or not, soon abbreviated to the I.G.B.) grew in proposed strength and representation. The merger of a private company and a royal college is not the simplest of local government operations.

It was a matter of vital importance to Miss Carroll and the council and one which was to demand their time and constant attention for many more years to come. But, having indicated the Northern's attitude, we can leave the negotiations for the moment confident that the school was anxious for a settlement which would safeguard its traditions. Though there was much speculation about proposals for a new college, it did not affect the daily lives of the students. Music was still the principal thing.

Adelaide Trainor, in charge of the speech and drama department, might have disagreed. The department was flourishing and it was necessary to find extra accommodation. (This was acquired at No. 89 Oxford Road, part of the same complex building.) On June 7, 1961, former students of the department founded "The Speech and Drama Association of the Northern School of Music", of which Miss Carroll was president and Miss Trainor chairman.

The annual drama production was of the morality play, *Everyman*, at Manchester Cathedral on March 16, 1961. Robert Hall reported:

> The production contained many interesting innovations, not the least effective of these being the use of a procession of monks bearing off the dead Everyman to the accompaniment of traditional plainsong (the *In Paradisum*). One must pay tribute to the fine co-operation of the music students under the direction of Miss Irene Wilde.

The annual opera venture was an ambitious double bill, produced by Sumner Austin and conducted by Aylmer Buesst. Weber's *Abu Hassan* seems to have given a bright start, for "the merry piece of nonsense was put over with great enjoyment by Alicia Robinson and Stephen Taylor in the two main singing parts". Weber was followed by Puccini's *Suor Angelica*. The title role was sung by Christina Morrison and that of the Princess by a promising young contralto, Alfreda Hodgson, who had originally joined the junior school. The cello had been her first study—she had won the prize for junior string players presented by Miss Carroll—but she had gone on to become a fine singer.

Douglas Wood, chorus master at the Royal Opera House, Covent Garden, was among lecturers at the holiday course. Others were Robin Wood (piano); Eric Thiman (conducting); and Leonard Hirsch (chamber music). The piano master classes were given by Louis Kentner.

Other musical events of the year included another performance of *The Canterbury Pilgrims* conducted by Read. The soloists were Christina Morrison, Stephen Taylor (tenor), and Malcolm Shaw. On November 21 the school's First Orchestra was invited to give a concert in the fine new hall of what was then the Royal College of Advanced Technology, Salford. Miss Carroll conducted the concert, which comprised

Malcolm Arnold's Scottish Dances, Schumann's *Rhenish* symphony, the Haydn trumpet concerto (soloist Geoffrey Boult) and the Bach A minor violin concerto (soloist Paul Buxton). On December 5 a series of three recitals by several promising students was begun. It was shared by Valerie Heath (piano) and Alfreda Hodgson.

The second recital, on January 30, 1962, was given by David Smith (piano), and Ian Rudge (cello), accompanied by Anne Stafford. The third was given on February 27 by Richard Walsh (piano) and Buxton, accompanied by John Wilson.

In April, the Hallé flautist William Morris, a member of the Northern School staff, was killed in a road accident. Miss Carroll noted : "Not only was Mr Morris a fine flautist and teacher of his instrument, but he was also beloved by everyone and everything. His visits to the school were very often quite brief ones between rehearsals and concerts at the Free Trade Hall, but he had always time to say a word and make us feel that he really belonged."

On May 24 the school orchestra returned to the Royal College of Advanced Technology, Salford, to give a concert in aid of the Hilda Collens memorial fund. This time the orchestra of sixty-four players, including a few former students, was conducted by Charles Groves. Herbert Winterbottom, a member of the O.S.A. who was then a member of the Salford college's technical staff, wrote that in Gordon Jacobs's trombone concerto "full justice was done by the soloist, John Iveson, who gave a most interesting and resourceful interpretation". In Bruch's violin concerto "the soloist was Colin Staveley,[1] whose sincere understanding of the work won prolonged acclamation".

Martha was chosen for the annual opera production, over which Sumner Austin and Aylmer Buesst again presided. Harriet Durham was sung by Tessa Hultgren, Plunkett by Stephen Taylor, and Nancy by Alfreda Hodgson. Ernest Read

---

[1] Staveley had been leader of the National Youth Orchestra.

conducted the choral and orchestral concert at the Houlds-
worth Hall on July 20. The main items were Elgar's *The
Music Makers,* Vaughan Williams's *Toward the Unknown
Region,* and Prokofiev's *Peter and the Wolf.*

The annual distribution of awards was held on October 30.
The chief guest was Dr W. Greenhouse Allt, Principal of
Trinity College of Music, who, after warning students against
becoming absorbed with the "strange new noises" of contem-
porary music, praised the work of Miss Carroll and suggested
that it would be "fitting" if Manchester University were to
bestow upon her the degree of Doctor of Music. The suggestion
was not taken up immediately by the university, but the 1964
New Year Honours List included Miss Carroll's name among
those awarded the O.B.E. Manchester's honorary M.A.
degree was conferred the following year, on July 8, 1965; on
March 23, 1966, Miss Carroll was elected an honorary
member of the Royal Academy of Music and on November
11, 1971, was made an honorary Fellow of the Manchester
Polytechnic. The honours were welcomed by the school
council as acknowledgment of Ida Carroll's services to music
and the school; Miss Carroll welcomed them as recognition of
the work of the Northern. The last word, however, is with the
chairman, Arthur J. Moon, as recorded in the minutes of the
council meeting held soon after the award of the O.B.E. It
states: "This acknowledgment of her great services to the
Northern School, and through it to the interests of music
throughout the country, gave the greatest pleasure to the
council, and the opportunity to record their own congratula-
tions and grateful thanks to Miss Carroll for the magnificent
services which this honour marks. They hope it has given her
an assurance that these services have been understood and
appreciated very widely, and that it will encourage and
sustain her through the stimulating but exacting operation of
leading the school successfully into the new organisation of
which it will be an essential part."

Note Moon's reference to the "stimulating and exacting

operation". Ever since talks began the Northern had been enthusiastic about a proposed new college, but the negotiations were not allowed to interfere with the school's academic and artistic progress. In December 1962 the school's performance of *Messiah* was conducted by Maurice Handford.[2] It was the beginning of an association with the Northern School which was to enrich Manchester's musical life for several years. At Salford, on March 12, 1963, the school orchestra gave its first concert under Handford's direction. The programme included the first performance in the North of England of five tableaux from Stravinsky's *Apollon Musagète,* the Liszt E flat piano concerto (soloist Richard Walsh), and Brahm's second symphony.

An old student, Marjorie G. Clough, described the concert as "a landmark, being the first of its kind since the orchestra had been taken over by a resident professional conductor. The great success of this policy was evident as the evening progressed. Between the audience and the orchestra was the dynamite of Mr Maurice Handford, quite apparent even from a back view. There was vivid life and music in every gesture; and with such a programme and performance obviously expected of them, the orchestra must have felt 'pros' indeed. Their conductor certainly treated them as such." Faults there may have been, but a lack of vitality does not seem to have been one of them.

A week later, on March 19, a coach full of students, staff, and friends left the Northern School and went south. They were "supporters" of Alfreda Hodgson who, accompanied by the pianist John Wilson, was making her London début that night, at the Wigmore Hall. After enjoying a recital which included Britten's song cycle, *Charm of Lullabies,* Op. 41, and a group of English songs, the Northernites returned tired but happy. Argo Ashton, one of the students who made the journey, recorded: "On returning to school soon after dawn, there was breakfast for us which had been generously prepared by Miss Carroll and the canteen staff." Miss Carroll had

[2] A former principal horn, Handford first conducted the Hallé in 1960 and frequently after that. Assistant Hallé conductor 1964, associate 1966–71.

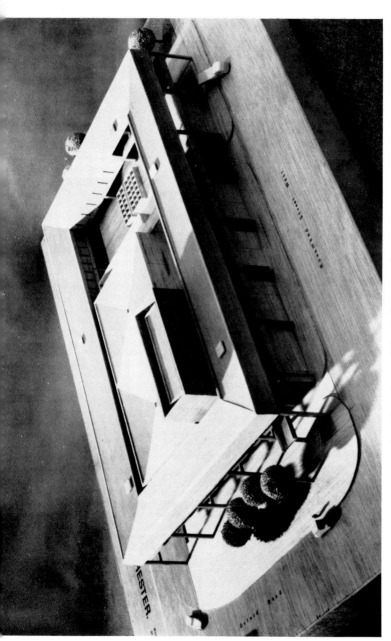

Architect's model of the new College

Ida Carroll
by Harold Riley

returned by train, and there she was, busy in the kitchen!

Aylmer Buesst conducted the school's production of *The Magic Flute* at the Lesser Free Trade Hall in July. Kay Fletcher sang Pamina, Stephen Taylor Tamino, Ian Comboy the Orator and Tessa Hultgren the Queen of the Night. The monster, revived after languishing in store since the school's production of 1955, again lived its little hour upon the stage before returning to what was described as "an obscure limbo". For the first time the holiday course was divided: after an opening recital by Janet Craxton and Alan Richardson of music for oboe and piano, one section went on to lectures and master classes given by Richardson, Douglas Robinson, Louis Kentner, and Gordon Clinton. The other part of the course, directed by Leonard Hirsch, comprised chamber and orchestral music.

Orchestral concerts during the 1963–4 season were again conducted by Handford, under whom "the orchestra has acquired a personality and is coping well with a regular concert repertoire".

The first concert, at Salford on November 19, was a Beethoven programme which included an impressive *Eroica* and a confident performance of the C minor piano concerto by David Smith. The second concert, also at Salford, included the Beethoven violin concerto played by the leader, Paul Buxton, Hindemith's *Nobilissima Visione*, and a suite from Bizet's *L'Arlésienne*. These two successful concerts were followed by a performance, at the Houldsworth Hall on December 10, of *The Dream of Gerontius*, in which the soloists were Alfreda Hodgson (contralto), Stephen Taylor (tenor), and Brian Fish (bass). The last concert of the term conducted by Handford was in aid of the Hilda Collens memorial fund. In addition to Mozart's twenty-ninth symphony, the programme included the first Manchester performance of Michael Tippett's oratorio, *A Child of Our Time*. The soloists were Alfreda Hodgson, Pauline Tinsley, Taylor, and Haskayne.

In the past the Northern School's reputation had been

H

established on the quality of the teachers it trained rather than on the evanescent stardom of performers. Miss Collens, whose main interest had been in the improvement of standards of music teaching, had been disinclined to "force" promising performers. She preferred to let them emerge and then encourage them. Many talented performers had indeed emerged, although it must be admitted that for budding soloists the Royal Manchester College of Music had for many years exerted a stronger fascination. Standards of the Northern's public concerts had been rising. The choir, first trained by Gertrude Riall and then by Irene Wilde, had always been good. The orchestra, trained by Handford, was gaining fluency and attracting favourable comment and much larger audiences.

In April 1964 the school's reputation for training fine performers was greatly enhanced when Alfreda Hodgson won the Kathleen Ferrier Memorial Scholarship and with it an invitation to give another Wigmore Hall recital and an engagement to sing at four concerts at the Royal Albert Hall under the direction of Sir Malcolm Sargent.

Because of the illness of his wife, Aylmer Buesst, who had conducted all the school's opera productions since they began in 1952, was unable to direct the performances of *Faust* given in the summer of 1964. His place was taken by Handford. Faust was sung by Stephen Taylor, Marguerite was sung on alternate evenings by Alison Hargan and Marie Dolan, Valentin by Peter Walker, Mephistopheles by Ian Comboy, and Siebel by Beryl Cook.

For the first time since the war there was no holiday course. For eight weeks from July to September two dozen workmen were removing the school's furniture, shifting files and pianos, and rearranging the accommodation as the school moved out of 89 and 91 and, after inevitable reshuffles of the premises in between, into No. 99 Oxford Road—a scheme which cost around £21,000. The main entrance was now in Sidney Street, but the Northern School safeguarded its more desirable Oxford Road address by having a letterbox let into the wall (built during the conversions) where No. 99 had been.

The premises at No. 91 were walled off and the demolition men moved in. Motorways wait for no man and for the next few years the music of the school was often accompanied by the sounds of pneumatic drills and cement mixers—later succeeded by the roar of car engines. (The drone of traffic was something they came to tolerate. The installation of traffic lights at the junction of Sidney Street and Oxford Road was to be a more serious distraction, for they would involve squealing brakes and revving engines. Fortunately for the general work of the school the main sufferers were only the Principal and the administrative staff—who had their being at that corner.)

In November three coachloads of staff and students travelled to London to take part in a performance of *Gerontius* which Handford conducted at the Duke's Hall of the Royal Academy of Music where he (an old student) was associate conductor of the First Orchestra. The Northern School Choir joined with the Orpington Junior Singers, the Thurrock Male Voice Choir, and the Strolling Players Orchestra. The soloists were Gerald English (tenor), Peter Walker, and Alfreda Hodgson.

On December 11 the school's drama students opened their new small theatre, which had been made possible by the recent rearrangements, with two plays by Christopher Fry, *The Boy with a Cart* and *A Phoenix Too Frequent*. The department acquitted itself well. Both plays were produced by Gerald McNally, a former student who had become a full-time member of staff. The staff had also been augmented by the appointment of Ronald Harvi of the B.B.C. as tutor in radio technique. There were also several visiting tutors. A third-year student of the department, Peter Williams, won the Guildhall School of Music's silver medal for gaining the highest total of marks in examinations for the licentiateship diploma.

Apart from the notable and deserved success of Alfreda Hodgson in winning the Ferrier award, old music students of the Northern were enhancing the school's reputation in many parts of the world. Frank Beevers was a music adviser in New Zealand, whence came tempting descriptions of sun and satisfaction. Margaret Gifford was enjoying life in Ghana; Margaret Leman (formerly Cardus) and Lydia Shaxon had settled in Australia, and so had Joan Lazaroff (formerly Farrow). Isabel Ward (formerly Hicks) seemed "to move above perpetually between different parts of the world". Many of these former students, as they worked and played their way round the world, kept in touch with the Northern. Their letters were sources of great satisfaction to Miss Carroll and her staff and also to most of the Northern's old students. In 1965 Judith Davis wrote from Prince George, Canada, where she was teaching music, to say:

> I had been warned that the children were acquainted almost solely with the Beatles and the like, but I took this with a pinch of salt. I breezed into the dimly-lit, ill-ventilated cellar known as the Bandroom, determined to teach a normal first aural training lesson; some ten minutes later there was a plaintive voice asking when we were going to learn about the Beatles! This attitude has continued but I think they are beginning to lose hope.

From the United States of America which he was touring with the London Symphony Orchestra, Colin Staveley wrote: "I enjoyed it enormously and learned a lot from playing with them. The first half of the U.S.A. tour was pretty grim, and involved long coach journeys each day (5–7 hours) and a concert most evenings in different provincial cities." Northern students contemplating an orchestral career would know what to expect.

Nearer at home other Northern students were advancing their careers, including Alfreda Hodgson, John Wilson (who was developing into one of Britain's finest accompanists), and other pianists who included Valerie Heath, David Smith (also a talented bassoonist), Graham Jackson, Hilarie Webster, and many others. Orchestral players gaining appointments were numerous. They included Gerald Brinnen, principal double-bass in the B.B.C. Symphony, Stephen Crabtree, principal double-bass with the Scottish National, and Derek Oldfield, who was musical director for a world tour undertaken by the Royal Shakespeare Company. Dorothy Pilling had several compositions published, Joan Spencer had a double-bass solo accepted by the Associated Board, and Sheila Middlebrooke had success with some of her flute pieces. Dr Annie Warburton was the author of authoritative textbooks on music. There was even a trend towards conducting : Michael Ashcroft became the first student to take a course of study leading to the L.R.A.M. diploma for choral conducting. An old student, John Crosdale, a former Hallé brass player, had attended a course at Tanglewood in 1959 at which the lecturers included Pierre Monteux and Aaron Copland. Crosdale is the conductor of several amateur orchestras in the North of England, including the Gorton Philharmonic.

With the deaths in 1965 of Myra Hess, the school's president, and Ernest Read the Northern lost two good friends. Read was, said Miss Carroll,

. . . from first to last a most helpful adviser, examiner, and friend. He will always be remembered as an outstanding musician, with a devotion to his job of giving enjoyment to young people through his concerts and orchestras, and with a fund of humour which was one of his greatest assets, to those with whom he came into contact. He looked for the good in a person and made allowance for any human weakness.

By June 1966, Miss Carroll was able to report :

This year has been the most crowded one in the life of the Northern School, not only physically but also in the performance of both music and drama. Never before have we been actually performing in one hall and rehearsing in another on the same night, but this has been the case recently. And because we have been increasing the number of public performances it does not mean that the teacher-training has been neglected. On the contrary, it is becoming more and more apparent that the one can help the other, and that the ideal training is for performance and teaching to run closely in harness, each making a full and worthwhile contribution to the other.

There was justifiable pride in the achievements of the school and its students. During the past twelve months there had been many successes: Ian Comboy had won a £450 Franckenstein Scholarship to study in Vienna for six months; Beryl Cook had won a £750 Stuyvesant Scholarship for a year at the London Opera Centre; and Alison Hargan, who had shown much promise as a soprano of great artistry, came second in the National Federation of Music Societies' Competition at Malvern in April 1966.

Apart from singers trained at the Northern, instrumentalists had joined various orchestras. The string players Paul Buxton, Gillian Holme, John Kenworthy, and Duncan Taylor were with the new B.B.C. Training Orchestra; Colin Staveley had become leader of the B.B.C. Welsh Orchestra; David Bagshaw (double bass) and Valerie Thompson (violin) had joined the Hallé; Allan Mead was second horn in the City of Birmingham Symphony Orchestra; and the bassoonist Avril Foster was with the Belfast Orchestra.

The number of teaching appointments ran into dozens. Among nearly forty old students who went to the trouble of notifying Miss Carroll of their posts, most of them were in Britain, although Margaret Gifford was starting the first Advanced level course in music for Africans in Kenya, Frank Beevers was director of music at Napier, in New Zealand, and Richard Walsh was professing the piano at Kingston

Music College, Jamaica. Old students were now so scattered about Britain and various parts of the world that the Old Students Association, besides considering holding regional meetings in Britain, was caused

> . . . to project our thoughts forward a few decades, and we find ourselves contemplating in imagination, without undue incredulity, possible future meetings taking place in various parts of the world, when we shall charter a jet plane as a kind of charabanc for the day. Australia, Africa and New Zealand seem well within our reach in these rosy dreams, and the U.S.A. seems positively suburban!

Wider still and wider.

The performance of music and drama during 1965–6 had deserved Miss Carroll's special mention. The speech and drama department, whose future as a separate school of acting had been under discussion since the autumn of 1964,[3] had given several productions, including Garcia Lorca's *The House of Bernarda Alba*, Wilde's *The Importance of Being Earnest, The Hollow Peace*, a programme of play extracts and dance drama based on the theme of war, and two plays for children which had been built up from improvisation before being scripted and produced.

Handford conducted the 1965 opera production, which was of *La Traviata*, with Violetta sung by Tessa Hultgren, and Alfredo by George Fisher. In March 1966 there were two studio performances (with John Wilson at the piano) of *Cosi fan tutte*. Concerts included a fine performance, at the Houldsworth Hall on December 10, 1965, of Elgar's *The Kingdom*, in which the soloists were Joan Aubin, Alison

---

[3] After discussion with J. P. Allen, of the Department of Education and Science, approaches were made to Manchester University and Granada Television, through the good offices of Sir Gerald Barry, about the possibility of co-operation in an arts centre. It was proposed that the department might become an integral part of such a centre. The centre has not yet materialised.

Hargan, George Fisher, and Leslie Auger. Of the orchestral concert conducted by Handford at Salford on March 15, 1966, Gloria Bakhshayesh (formerly Bradley) wrote:

The overture to Schubert's *Rosamunde* was followed by two Mozart arias sung by Ian Comboy. Here the orchestra provided a very unwieldy and cumbersome accompaniment but, despite this disadvantage, Ian Comboy projected his fine, resonant bass voice very well. Neville Duckworth then played the Second Clarinet Concerto of Weber, executing the quicker passages with great brilliance and achieving a beautiful, smooth tone in the slow movement. The concert ended with a very fine performance of Borodin's Second Symphony.

The year 1966 is to be remembered not just for the appearance of the oboist Leon Goossens at the holiday course, or for production of *The Marriage of Figaro*. The most significant event was the signing of the agreement establishing the Northern College of Music, Manchester. The first meeting of the interim governing body, or I.G.B., had been held as early as 1962 and there had been hopes that work on building the new college might begin in the 1964–5 financial year. But there had been complications about finance and related problems, including the compulsory purchase of a site in Oxford Road. The architect, W. H. Allen, had been contemplating completion not later than 1967, but the course of this marriage of convenience between the two colleges had not run smooth. The issues involved were much too complex to make satisfactory solutions easy to arrive at, but there was a determination by all concerned in the discussions that agreement should not be sacrificed on the altar of speed. It was better that the committee-work diplomacy should arrive at harmony than that the pressures of a deadline should make themselves felt. A house divided against itself cannot stand; the foundations of a new music college must needs be free of schism.

CHAPTER TWELVE

A New Beginning

Two die, and one is born.
Hail and farewell;
Let mourning organ swell,
And heralding trumpets play:
The best Tomorrow has its roots
In Yesterday.

—Thomas Pitfield, composer and professor of composition at the Royal Manchester College of Music, on the laying of the foundation stone of the Northern College of Music, April 1, 1971.

Agreement on the creation of a new college of music having been reached and the documents signed, there were still administrative problems for the transitional period. Salaries and appointment of staff from now on would need to be considered with special care: what were the present needs of the Northern and the R.M.C.M., and what effect would any decision taken now have on the new college? With the assumption by the Department of Education and Science of financial responsibility for the Northern, the R.M.C.M., and the new college, the interim governing body was translated into a joint committee, fully capitalised and with impressive powers.

The first meeting of the joint committee was held at Manchester Town Hall on October 27, 1966. Sir Maurice Pariser, of Manchester City Council, was elected chairman. The Northern had four representatives: Arthur J. Moon, the chairman; Albert Hague, the honorary treasurer; and council members Philip Lockley and John Padmore. The R.M.C.M. also had four representatives, Lancashire six, Cheshire four, Manchester four, Salford two, and Manchester University one. There were also representatives of the B.B.C., the Hallé, the Royal Liverpool Philharmonic, and the Arts Council. Percy Lord, who arranged the original discussions several years before, was co-opted as a foundation member. Simon Towneley, formerly chairman of the I.G.B. (who had joined the Northern School council earlier in the year), was co-opted a member of the sub-committees responsible for staffing and building.

From September 1967 the financial affairs of the Northern School and the Royal College were the responsibility of the joint committee and, whatever their feelings about the "fusion" and the loss of independence, members of the Northern's staff were delighted to receive increases in pay soon after. Their salaries were brought more into line with those received by teachers in other fields of education. The salaries were paid on behalf of the joint committee by Manchester city treasurer's department with funds provided by the parties involved, including the Department of Education and Science. Even though Government-imposed restrictions on public as well as private spending, caused the new college to be omitted from the 1968–9 building programme, it was realised that something would turn up soon—a far cry from the days of 1955 when Miss Collens did not know where the next penny was coming from or, indeed, whether there would be another penny. In 1969 a tender of £828,299 from H. Fairweather & Co. Ltd. was approved and building began on November 10, for completion within twenty-seven months. The Northern College of Music, Manchester, was to open in 1972.

There was the remaining question of appointing a Principal. The Northern School's view all along was that a "neutral" Principal—one owing allegiance neither to the school nor the Royal College—should be appointed. This was, as we have seen, almost certainly one of the reasons behind the Northern School council's delay in appointing Ida Carroll after Miss Collens's death in 1956, when the idea of a new college was beginning to gain ground.

The post was advertised in 1969 and a short list was prepared. The R.M.C.M. Principal, Frederic Cox, had applied, and so had Ida Carroll. In such circumstances, the appointment of either could not be considered a serious possibility. A further short list was prepared and John Manduell, director of music at Lancaster University, was appointed Principal-designate. He took up his duties on September 1, 1971.

In September 1970 Cox resigned his post and became Principal Emeritus of the R.M.C.M., Dr John Wray acting as Principal. Miss Carroll remained as active as ever and she dismissed any speculation about her retirement by her readiness to join Manduell's staff.

The negotiations were long and difficult. Despite the rivalry, there was goodwill on all sides. But Miss Carroll, who had been devoted to Miss Collens and her school, was resolute in fighting off any suggestions of a takeover by the Royal Manchester College of Music. She sometimes seemed stubborn, at least to those with whom she disagreed. She disliked red tape, preferring what she preferred to call "green elastic". Her decision to press on with proposals for a new college involved her in countless hours of meetings, letter-writing, and what to most other people would have been an intolerable administrative burden. It is unlikely that Miss Collens, who much preferred teaching to the tyranny of paperwork, would have coped so successfully with the problems which arose after 1955. Resolute she certainly was also, but she seems to have been something of an introvert.

Miss Carroll, whose personality is more outward-looking, seems to have enjoyed the negotiations. Once a satisfactory agreement had been reached, she seems to have been inspired by the idea that the Northern School should play a vital part in something entirely new. Her enthusiasm has not been confined to the planning of the new college, however. In these last years of an independent Northern School she has guided it towards standards higher than at any time in its existence.

In the last few years, the Northern School has answered

decisively critics who felt that standards of performance were low. Public concerts have been noticeably ambitious, and usually ambition had been accompanied by technical and artistic excellence. On November 30, 1967, the Northern School of Music choir, long the finest choir in the greater Manchester area, at last appeared at a Hallé concert when Maurice Handford conducted Stravinsky's *Perséphone*. This was followed by other Hallé appearances including the memorable concert performances, in May 1968, conducted by Sir John Barbirolli, of *Otello* and, as part of the Berlioz centenary celebrations, in *L'Enfance du Christ,* and a concert performance of *Les Troyens*.[1] Under Handford the school had distinguished itself with many other notable performances, including that of Elgar's *The Apostles* on February 23, 1967, when the soloists at the Free Trade Hall were Pauline Tinsley and Alfreda Hodgson, with the male parts sung by Ellis Keeler, Stephen Taylor, Peter Walker, and James Calladine.

To the record of these memorable years must also be added mention of fine performances of Beethoven's *Missa Solemnis,* Handel's *Messiah,* and Walton's *Belshazzar's Feast,* all conducted by Handford. Also under Handford the school opera productions gained in technical assurance. In the 1967 production of *Idomeneo,* George Fisher sang the title role, Ilia was sung by Ruth Williams, Electra by Valerie Whalley, Idamente by Patrick Broderick. It is a difficult opera to realise successfully and it seemed that the school had overreached itself; but the 1968 production of *Hugh the Drover* was one of the finest of this Vaughan Williams opera ever staged. The title role was sung by Trefor Davies and Mary by Delcie Tetsill. Gluck's *Alcestis* was chosen for the following year: the name part was sung on alternate nights by Diane Mansfield and Angela Sorrigan. Trefor Davies sang Admetus.

On Sunday, July 6, 1969, Ida Carroll and her sister Elsa were hosts at a London hotel to a large gathering of friends

---

[1] *L'Enfance* was given at the Free Trade Hall on December 12, 1968, and *Les Troyens* in two parts on April 10 and 17, 1969. Handford conducted both works.

who then went on to a service to mark the centenary of the birth of Walter Carroll. The service at the Church of the Holy Sepulchre, Without Newgate, was attended by friends from many parts of Britain. Music from that service was repeated the following Tuesday at St Ann's Parish Church, Manchester. The Northern School choir sang at both services and the organist was Herbert Winterbottom, who was now director of music at Salford University and who had succeeded William Hardwick (organ teacher at the Northern until his death in 1968) as the church organist at St Ann's.

The school began its golden jubilee celebrations early—on October 28, 1969, with the annual distribution of awards at the Houldsworth Hall. The chairman was Arthur J. Moon and the presentations were made by Kathleen Ollerenshaw, chairman of Manchester education committee and also of the joint committee of the Northern College. At the reception held afterwards at the Midland Hotel, Dr Ollerenshaw formally presented honorary Fellowship of the school to Geoffrey Griffiths, the bursar.

On November 18 Handford conducted the school orchestra in a concert at Salford University, as the Royal College of Advanced Technology was now styled. The programme comprised music by Arnold, Brahms, Grieg, and Beethoven's seventh symphony. A second concert at Salford, on February 3, included Dvořák's eighth symphony, Op. 88, Mozart's twenty-ninth, and Haydn's violin concerto in F played by David Ogden, with John Wilson at the harpsichord.

On May 19 Handford conducted a performance at the Free Trade Hall of Vaughan Williams's *Pilgrim's Progress*. Soloists taking part included Alfreda Hodgson and Delcie Tetsill, John Noble (Pilgrim), Ian Comboy, Josephine Adams, and Ellis Keeler. The large orchestra was led by Maurice Clare.

May also had its lively social side, including the school football club's annual dinner at the Grand Hotel. It followed a good season, in which the Northern had played many matches and, even in defeat, had never failed to score. The team captain, Brian Scott, led the scoring with twenty goals. He was presented with a silver cup by the club president, Miss Carroll. She had followed the season with great interest and may be presumed to have found satisfaction in the team's nine–one victory over the Royal Manchester College of Music team. The club thus ended its days on a note of triumph, for it merged with its defeated rivals to form the Northern College of Music Association Football Club, which has since gone on to triumph over two other music colleges.

In July Handford conducted the school production of *The Magic Flute*: Diane Mansfield was the Queen of the Night; Trefor Davies sang Tamino; Diane Wolstencroft Pamina; and William Hill Sarastro. With Mozart completed, the school set about the round of social events which built towards the climax of the golden jubilee. They began on Tuesday, July 21, with a civic reception given at Manchester Town Hall by the Lord Mayor, Councillor William Downward. Those at the reception included Miss Carroll, members of the school council, final-year students, old students, and local authority education officers. Among those who sent messages of congratulation was Sir John Barbirolli, Conductor Laureate of the Hallé Orchestra.[2] The next night a golden jubilee dance was held at the Grand Hotel; Thursday was spent on a coach trip to Chatsworth House and a tour of Derbyshire.

The celebrations on July 24 began with a lunch given by Miss Carroll at the Midland Hotel. It was followed by a thanksgiving service at St Ann's Parish Church conducted by the rector, Canon Eric Saxon, who dedicated a window[3] in memory of Hilda Collens. From St Ann's Church, the guests took a short break, and then went on to Friends' Meeting House in Mount Street for a recital in which Kendall Taylor played Beethoven's piano sonatas Opp. 109, 110 and 111. The last event of the golden jubilee was an old students' dinner

---

[2] It was one of his last kindnesses. He died a week later, on July 29, 1970.
[3] The window is the work of Alan Boyson.

at the Grand Hotel. Because of the celebrations—and the consequent need for rest—there was no holiday course that summer.

Although the days of the Northern School of Music as a
separate institution were numbered, the 1970–1 academic
year showed no loss of vigour or enterprise. The first major
event was the distribution of awards at the Houldsworth Hall
when the guest speaker was J. S. B. Boyce, successor to the
late Sir Percy Lord as chief education officer of Lancashire.
On March 25 the school mounted a concert performance at
the Free Trade Hall of *The Damnation of Faust* by Berlioz.
The day before, Alfreda Hodgson, who was to have sung
Marguerite, went down with influenza and Miss Carroll spent
hours phoning friends all over Britain in the hope of finding
a replacement. Eventually, Maureen Guy, rehearsing at Aber-
deen with Alexander Gibson, agreed to fly down to Manchester and, after only one rehearsal, sang the part and
contributed to a successful concert.

The other principals were Trefor Davies (Faust), Ray Clarke
(Brander), and Albert Haskayne (Mephistopheles). The
conductor was Charles Groves.

The following week, on a cold and gloomy first of April, the
foundation stone of the Northern College of Music was
formally laid and unveiled amid the shell of steel and concrete
now arising from the site in Oxford Road. Frederic Cox and
Ida Carroll pulled together on the curtain cord and the stone
bearing the names of both, was revealed. Each made a brief
address. In hers, Miss Carroll said:

It is a long time since November 1955, which was the
date of the first talks with the chief education officer in
Manchester about the future of the Northern School of
Music, but the time has passed remarkably quickly because
the subsequent talks have brought closer a project in music
which must be entirely unique in this country.

I have found the exercise profoundly interesting, and
there can be no-one who feels more joy in the knowledge

that, despite national crises and the sad passing of many of the original planners, such as Sir Percy Lord, Alderman Mrs Fletcher, and Mr Clement Gerrard, the new Northern College of Music is rising from the ground and will shortly be completed as a training ground for musicians of all kinds, performers and teachers, in the future.

It is not my job to commend individually all the people who have contributed to this new college of music, but I must express my thanks to Mr Boyce, who stepped into Sir Percy Lord's place; my present chairman, Mr Jack Moon; and also to Mr Frederic Cox, who has been my partner in many of the discussions.

The four local education authorities of Lancashire, Cheshire, Manchester, and Salford, with the Department of Science and Technology, have all helped to make this college possible, and I can see nothing but good in the future, if the best traditions and goodwill of the present colleges are allowed to go forward into the new college and so strengthen its growth. There must be some spiritual chord which draws us together at this historic moment and, in helping Mr Cox to lay this foundation stone, it is my sincere wish that the members of staff and the students will give to our new Principal, Mr John Manduell, the loyal support that it has been my privilege to enjoy for many years.

It was then left to the builders and contractors to press on with the new college, with its provision for an 800-seat theatre, a dual-purpose concert and assembly hall for 500, a recital room to seat 200–250 people, a large lecture room, a library, an organ, and 90 individual tutorial rooms.

At the Northern School, preparations continued for the July production by Sumner Austin of Verdi's *Nabucco,* conducted by James Robertson, of the London Opera Centre. It was one of the best operatic productions ever staged by the school.

As the new Northern College of Music was due to open in the autumn of 1972, the distribution of awards at the Houldsworth Hall on October 18, 1971, was the last of an independent Northern School. The chief guest was James Loughran who the previous month had taken up his duties as the Hallé's principal conductor, the first time that a Hallé conductor had made the annual prize presentations. Loughran also presented, at a ceremony held afterwards at the Midland Hotel, honorary Fellowships of the Northern School to Albert Hague, the honorary treasurer, Alfreda Hodgson, and John Wilson.

In her annual report, Ida Carroll was, as always, looking forward to the future. The main doubts concerned the future of the school's 700 part-time students. In the previous month the students had been notified that the part-time department would close in July 1972, as a result of the creation of the new college (which is mainly for full-time students). It had been understood by the Northern School, throughout the long years of negotiation, that its part-time work would be catered for by the local education authorities. Up to the time of the annual distribution, only Salford had made provision for the senior and junior part-timers of the Northern School, regardless of where they might live. At the time of writing, proposals by other authorities were still under discussion.

The question of the part-time department was the darkest cloud to cast its shadow. As the school looked not to death but to transfiguration as a vital part of the new college, there were many rays of warm sunshine, including the success, as performers, of two more Northern singers : Alison Hargan won the Stuyvesant Scholarship and was now with Welsh National Opera, and Diane Mansfield won the £1,000 Marion Countess of Harewood Scholarship for study at the London Opera Centre. With thoughts of *Der Freischütz*, the Verdi *Requiem*, and a graduation ball still to come, the school is crowding its last year of independent life. Even when the marriage contract between the Northern School and the

I

R.M.C.M. formally becomes effective in September 1972, the school's diploma courses will continue until completion within the new college. The Northern's premises in Oxford Road are also likely to be needed during the transitional period.

Eventually, when the great changes are complete, approximately 160 students of the new college—one third of the total—will be from the Northern School. Whether that qualifies the school for an entry in many well-known reference books from which it is now omitted matters little. From its earliest days, when there was a nucleus of only nine students, right up to the 1950s, the school did not always receive the recognition it deserved. Occasionally this was of great concern to Miss Collens, especially when she was striving to resolve the problem of graduate status. It involved the career and salary prospects of her old students, for in the highly competitive world of music and music-teaching the reputation of being a second-class college producing second-class musicians was not one which Miss Collens could allow. Such a reputation would have closed the Northern within a year.

It was as a teacher that Hilda Collens found her vocation and it was in training other musicians to be good teachers that she found fulfilment. Whatever the gibes about those who teach, Miss Collens recognised that dedicated and well-trained teachers could be a powerful factor in the furtherance of music and its appreciation.

Teachers, however, rarely win the big prizes. They are content to see their pupils win them. Miss Collens shied away from publicity, she received no public honours, and she amassed no fortune. The men who headed Britain's other colleges of music might have been amused had they known that on Friday afternoons Hilda Collens would slip out to do some weekend shopping for herself and her elderly mother. Yet Miss Collens, having bought her provisions and thinking ahead to her Sunday Bible classes, was not without pride in the Northern's achievements. She would often state publicly the number of teaching appointments gained by old students and make a conservative guess at the number of pupils they taught and influenced. She ensured that the school magazine recorded the Northern's many successes. If in retrospect some of these successes—a recital here, a lecture there—seem trivial, it is only because the Northern's subsequent expansion, with ever-rising standards, make them seem so now. At the time when the school was struggling to survive they were very important.

Miss Collens and her staff were justifiably proud that the Northern produced so many excellent music teachers, but there is the debit side. Because the school had built up a reputation for training teachers, because Miss Collens shunned the limelight, and because the school had slender financial resources, first-class performers tended to look else-where for help in their careers.

The training of performing musicians was never one of the Northern School's primary aims. Until the end of the Second World War there were very few male students, and even in 1972 men were marginally outnumbered by the Northern's women students. Lack of money hindered diversification and restrained Miss Collen's ambitions for further expansion. Towards the end of her life, when the school's reputation for teacher-training was firmly established, she was often urged to increase the range of activities by those who knew little of the enormous risks such expansion would involve. In her last years Miss Collens, although she was as sympathetic as ever to widening the Northern's scope, concentrated on the formidable task of making the school a viable enterprise. That could be done only by following policies which had been proved sound. The training of music teachers remained the most important thing, and it attracted those who wished to teach rather than those who aspired to fame as opera singers, concert pianists, or virtuoso violinists.

In recent years, when the school has become more confident of the future and more certain of its financial support, there has indeed been much greater emphasis on the performance of music. Sometimes ambition has outrun the resources available to a small school, but standards have been rising steadily as students gain much-needed experience. Not only has the choir maintained its supremacy, but the Northern is able to call on the musicianship of a growing number of gifted (and well trained) solo singers and instrumentalists.

A steady flow of performers as well as teachers graduate from the Northern School each year. If one needs living monuments to the school's endeavour one has only to look around: schools throughout the world have music teachers who trained at the Northern, many of Britain's orchestras include Northern players, and the whole world of music is the oyster for the "family" Miss Collens started. It is wrong, really, to write of monuments, no matter how much alive, or of epitaphs. The Northern has been, and still is, a creative force. The drama school of Manchester Polytechnic is a cutting which has taken root strongly: it came from good Northern stock. The Northern College of Music came into being as a result of the Northern School's search for security and its willingness to co-operate with the Royal Manchester College of Music as an equal partner.

The discussions which led to the creation of the new college were undertaken by the Northern School with a spirit of adventure and an unshakeable faith in the future. The traditions begun by Miss Collens have been continued by Miss Carroll. The "family" has grown but its spirit of friendship endures. Miss Carroll once said: "I don't worry about things. I know they'll be all right. Something has always helped us. We've had the luck because we've had the faith."

Appendix 1

CHRONOLOGY

This chronology is a selection of some of the more important events, leavened by a few of the less significant. The object is to give an idea of the increasing range of the Northern School's activities over the years.

1920   Matthay School of Music, Manchester branch, founded.

1923   Move from Hime and Addison's to Tudor Galleries, Deansgate.

1927   Move to 260 Deansgate.

1934   Move to Oxford Road.

1937   Annual orchestral concert conducted by William Rees. Beethoven's Emperor concerto played by Myra Scott. Master classes by Clifford Curzon.

1938   Orchestral concert, Houldsworth Hall, conducted by William Rees. Programme included Beethoven's first symphony, and a Mozart concerto and Bach's great unaccompanied chaconne, soloist Maurice Clare (violin).

1939   21st anniversary of the Manchester holiday course on Music.

1941   21st anniversary of the Matthay School, Manchester.

1943   The Northern School of Music, Manchester, incorporated.

1946   Myra Hess President.

1949   *Messiah*, Albert Hall, November 17, conductor Ernest Read. Soloists Joan Moss, Hazel Pullen, Vincent Coates, and James Calladine. Orchestra led by Reginald Stead.

1950   *The Creation*, Albert Hall, Manchester, May 25, conductor Ernest Read. Joan Moss, Vincent Coates, and James Calladine.

Messiah, Albert Hall, December 4, conductor Ernest Read. Orchestra led by Arthur Percival. Soloists Joan Moss, Norah Grayson, Vincent Coates, James Calladine.

1951 Junior School concert, Houldsworth Hall, June 23. Orchestral instruments included for the first time.

1952 Burnham Committee approves graduate status for Northern School students "who fulfil the special conditions established by the school".

Elijah, Albert Hall, March 3, conductor Ernest Read. Soloists Joan Moss, Patricia Wallace, Vincent Coates, and Albert Haskayne. Senior School orchestra led by Arthur Percival.

First opera production, Lesser Free Trade Hall, Manchester, July 2 and 3, *The Bartered Bride.* Producer Sumner Austin, conductor Aylmer Buesst.

1953 *Die Fledermaus,* four performances, Lesser Free Trade Hall, July. Producer Sumner Austin, conductor Aylmer Buesst.

1954 Recital of chamber music by members of the Senior School, Houldsworth Hall, June 3. Programme includes movements from Mendelssohn's Octet, Brahms's String Sextet, Op. 36, and other works by Haydn, Bach, and Vaughan Williams.

The Marriage of Figaro, Lesser Free Trade Hall, July 8–10. Producer Sumner Austin, conductor Aylmer Buesst.

1955 *Messiah,* Houldsworth Hall, March 17, conductor Ernest Read. Soloists Pamela Rhodes, Patricia Wallace, John O'Sullivan, and Albert Haskayne.

Junior School's first orchestral concert, Houldsworth Hall, March 18, conductor Ida Carroll. Programme includes Mendelssohn's G minor piano concerto, soloist Victoria Sumner.

The Magic Flute, Lesser Free Trade Hall, July 5–8. Producer Sumner Austin, conductor Aylmer Buesst.

String Orchestra concert, Houldsworth Hall, July 20, conductor Ida Carroll. Programme includes Walter Leigh's Concertante for piano and strings, soloist Terence Taylor.

1956 *Elijah,* Houldsworth Hall, February 27, conductor Charles Groves. Soloists Grace Yerkess, Patricia Wallace, John Hughes, and Albert Haskayne.
Hilda Collens dies, April 28.
The Merry Wives of Windsor, Lesser Free Trade Hall, July 4–7.

1957 *The Creation,* Houldsworth Hall, March 27, conductor Ernest Read. Soloists Norma Day, George Ward, and Albert Haskayne. Organist William Hardwick.
Mignon, Lesser Free Trade Hall, July 3–6.
The Snow Queen, Lesser Free Trade Hall, November 26 and 27, a production by the speech and drama department.

1958 Ida Carroll appointed Principal, March 31.
The Canterbury Pilgrims, Houldsworth Hall, May 15, conductor Ernest Read. Soloists Eileeen O'Neill, Stephen Crabtree, and John Shaw.
The Daughter of the Regiment, Lesser Free Trade Hall, July 2–5.

1959 *The Witnesses,* by Clive Sansom, a speech and drama presentation, Manchester Cathedral, May 7.
L'Elisir d'Amore, Lesser Free Trade Hall, July 1–4.
First honorary Fellowships.

1960 40th anniversary.
The Bartered Bride, Lesser Free Trade Hall, July 6–9.

1961 *Everyman,* speech and drama production, Manchester Cathedral, March 16.
Abu Hassan and *Suor Angelica,* Lesser Free Trade Hall, July 5–8.
Orchestral concert, Salford, November 21, conductor Ida Carroll.

Arms and the Man, speech and drama production, November 30–December 2.

1962   Orchestral concert, Salford, conductor Charles Groves. *Martha,* Lesser Free Trade Hall, July 4–7.

Choral and orchestral concert, Houldsworth Hall, July 20, conductor Ernest Read. Programme includes *The Music Makers* and *Toward the Unknown Region.*

1963   Orchestral concert, Salford, March 12, conductor Maurice Handford. Programme includes the first performance in the North of England of Stravinsky's *Apollon Musagète.*

Much Ado About Nothing, speech and drama production, May 29 and 30.

The Magic Flute, Lesser Free Trade Hall, July 3–6, conductor Aylmer Buesst.

Annual holiday course divided: one part for master classes and lectures, the other for chamber and orchestral music.

Choral and orchestral concert, Houldsworth Hall, June 14, conductor Maurice Handford. Programme includes Bruckner *Te Deum.* Soloists Alison Hargan, Stephen Taylor, and Brian Fish.

The Dream of Gerontius, Houldsworth Hall, December 10, conductor Maurice Handford. Soloists Alfreda Hodgson, Stephen Taylor, and Brian Fish.

1964   Orchestral concert, Salford, March 3, conductor Maurice Handford. Programme includes Hindemith's *Nobilissima Visione.*

Choral and orchestral concert, Salford, May 12, conductor Maurice Handford. Programme includes first Manchester performance of Tippett's *A Child of Our Time.* Soloists Pauline Tinsley, Alfreda Hodgson, Stephen Taylor, and Brian Fish.

Shakespearean programme, a combined presentation by the music and drama departments, Lesser Free Trade Hall, June 4–6.

Faust, Lesser Free Trade Hall, July 2–4, producer Sumner Austin, conductor Maurice Handford.

Orchestral concert, Salford, November 10, conductor Maurice Handford. Programme includes Rachmaninov's C minor piano concerto, soloist David Smith.

School choir in *The Dream of Gerontius,* Royal Academy of Music, November 28.

Choral and orchestral concert, Houldsworth Hall, December 4, conductor Maurice Handford. Programme includes Bruckner's setting of Psalm 150 and the third Mass, in F minor.

New studio theatre opened by drama department, December 11, with two plays by Christopher Fry, *The Boy with a Cart* and *A Phoenix Too Frequent.*

1965   Violin and piano sonatas played by Maurice Clare and John Wilson, at the school, February 8.

String Orchestra concert, Houldsworth Hall, February 16, conductor Leonard Hirsch.

Amici Quartet recital at the school, March 2. Programme includes Bartok's sixth quartet.

Holst concert, Houldsworth Hall, May 18, conductor Maurice Handford. *St Paul's Suite for Strings, Hymn of Jesus,* and the *Choral Symphony.*

La Traviata, Lesser Free Trade Hall, June 30–July 3, conductor Maurice Handford.

The Kingdom, Houldsworth Hall, December 10, conductor Maurice Handford. Soloists Alison Hargan, Joan Aubin, George Fisher, and Leslie Auger.

1966   Orchestral concert, Salford, March 15, conductor Maurice Handford. Programme includes Weber's second clarinet concerto, soloist Neville Duckworth, and Bruckner's second symphony.

Cosi fan tutte, studio performances, March 17 and 18.

The Marriage of Figaro, Lesser Free Trade Hall, June 28–July 2, conductor Maurice Handford.

K

1967   *The Apostles,* Free Trade Hall, February 23, conductor Maurice Handford. Soloists Pauline Tinsley, Alfreda Hodgson, Stephen Taylor, Ellis Keeler, Peter Walker, and James Calladine.

      Rural Music Schools Association annual course, director Bernard Shore, at the school for the holiday course.

      Idomeneo, Lesser Free Trade Hall, July, conductor Maurice Handford.

      School choir takes part in Hallé performance of Stravinsky's *Perséphone,* Free Trade Hall, November 30, conductor Maurice Handford.

1968   *Missa Solemnis,* Free Trade Hall, April 2, conductor Maurice Handford, Soloists Rae Woodland, Alfreda Hodgson, Malcolm Lea, and Peter Walker.

      School choir takes part in three Hallé concert performances of *Otello,* May, Sir John Barbirolli's silver jubilee programme in Manchester and Sheffield.

      Hugh the Drover, Lesser Free Trade Hall, July 10–13, conductor Maurice Handford.

      Autumn. Drama department becomes part of Manchester College of Art and Design (now part of Manchester Polytechnic).

      Messiah, Houldsworth Hall, December 10, conductor Maurice Handford. Soloists Delcie Tetsill, Alfreda Hodgson, Malcolm Lea, and Peter Walker.

      School choir in Hallé performance of *L'Enfance du Christ,* Free Trade Hall, December 12, conductor Maurice Handford.

1969   March 25, Free Trade Hall, choral and orchestral concert, conductor Maurice Handford. Programme comprises Bruckner's Mass in E minor and the *Te Deum,* and Walton's *Belshazzar's Feast.* Soloists include Delcie Tetsill, Judith Mackenzie, Trefor Davies, Kieran McNiff, and Peter Walker.

June 24, school recital room, concert of original compositions by students.

Alcestis, Lesser Free Trade Hall, July 9–12, conductor Maurice Handford.

Messiah, Free Trade Hall, December 2, conductor Maurice Handford.

1970 Golden jubilee year.

February 1, school choir in Hallé performance of Haydn's *St Nicholas Mass,* Free Trade Hall, conductor Maurice Handford, contralto soloist Alfreda Hodgson. Orchestral concert, Salford, February 3, conductor Maurice Handford.

The Pilgrim's Progress, concert performance, Free Trade Hall, May 19, conductor Maurice Handford. Soloists included Josephine Adams, Alfreda Hodgson, Trefor Davies, John Noble, and Ian Comboy.

The Magic Flute, Lesser Free Trade Hall, July, conductor Maurice Handford.

1971 *The Damnation of Faust,* Free Trade Hall, March 25, conductor Charles Groves. Soloists included Maureen Guy (Marguerite), Albert Haskayne (Mephistopheles), and Ray Clarke (Brander).

Nabucco, Lesser Free Trade Hall, July 7–10, conductor James Robertson.

1972 Orchestral concert, Salford, February 15, conductor Maurice Clare.

Verdi's *Requiem,* Free Trade Hall, March 7, conductor James Robertson. Soloists Alison Hargan, Vyna Martin, Trefor Davies, and Ray Clarke.

Der Freischütz, Lesser Free Trade Hall, June 21–24 (planned), conductor James Robertson.

Graduate status was approved in 1952, although external

examinations were taken from the school's earliest years. The numbers of successes to August 2, 1971, are:

> G.N.S.M. 395 in all
> A.N.S.M. 68
> L.R.A.M., A.R.C.M., L.T.C.L., L.G.S.M.,
> A.R.C.O., etc. 1,895

Appendix 2

Fellowship of the Northern School of Music:

1959	1	Ida Carroll
	2	Doris M. Euerby
	3	Beatrice Rollins (died 1967)
1960	4	Eileen Chadwick
	5	Dorothy Pilling
	6	Marjorie Proudlove
	7	Adelaide Trainor
	8	Irene Wilde
1961	9	Elizabeth Bellamy
	10	Edna Jamieson (now Hall)
	11	Constance Kay
	12	Leonard Latchford
	13	Mary Dunkerley (now Lockley)
	14	Gertrude Riall (now Bromley)
	15	Annie O. Warburton (now Hawkins)
1963	16	Albert Haskayne
	17	Herbert Winterbottom
1964	18	Alice Thompson
1966	19	Anne Brindley
	20	Arthur Burgan
	21	Gerald Brinnen
	22	Terence Taylor
1968	23	Peter Salt
1969	24	Geoffrey Griffiths
1971	25	Albert Hague
	26	Alfreda Hodgson (now Blissett)
	27	John Wilson

INDEX

BRUCE L DOUGLAS

NORTHERN SCHOOL OF MUSIC